Honest With God: Reflections
On Faith and Doubt

Mel Leaman

HONEST WITH GOD: Reflections On Faith And Doubt
Copyright © 2017 by Mel Leaman.

All rights reserved. Printed in the United States of America. No part of this book may be used or reproduced in any manner whatsoever without written permission except in the case of brief quotations embodied in critical articles or reviews.

ISBN-13: 978-1973935575
ISBN-10: 1973935570

First Edition: July, 2017

TABLE OF CONTENTS

Acknowledgements vii
Introduction 9
A Bigger Brain or a Different Being? 13
A Black Jesus 15
Conditioned by Racism and Called to Reconciliation (2009) 17
A Burning Love 23
A Choice and A Curse 25
A New Twist on What We Treasure 27
A Strange Messiah 28
Baptism of Love 30
Let's Drink to That! (2006) 31
Being Still: Is God Safe? 34
Get Me to the Quiet (2010) 35
Blaming and Scapegoating the Poor 37
Buy Me Some Poverty 39
Called and Clueless 41
Can I be a Man of God? (April 6, 2000) 41
Can A Non-Christian Abide in That Love? 43
Can A Prisoner Be Free? 45
Can't Face Those Demons Alone 47
Mercy and Forgiveness 50

Choices Come with Shadows	56
Compassion, Justice, and Borg	58
Contentment In Plenty and Want	60
Create A Clean Heart	62
Vanquished in 2005	63
Depart from Evil; Pursue Good	66
Devoted to the One I Despise	67
Scaring Myself: A Crazy Kind of Communion (2005)	68
Dominion and the Divine Image	70
Don't Bungle This One	72
Promises to Remember (2006)	73
Over "This?" (1999)	74
Dumb Reasoning	76
Please Sarah, Don't Laugh (2010)	77
Duty and Reward	81
Ecological Justice	83
Brethos (2006)	85
Our House (1997)	86
Elemental Spirits	87
Embracing the Shadow	88
Who Can Rouse the Deadly Silence:	89
Envy and "The Other"	94
Footwashing: Body and Soul	95
Forbidden Flesh: Can't Touch This!	98
The Folly Of Never	99
Praise of Sexuality	100
Joy of Man's Desiring (2010)	101
From First Kiss to Faltering Faith	104

Handle with Care	107
Here Comes That Dreamer!	109
Hubris, Humility, and the Heart	111
It's Second Nature to Me Now	113
Jesus Vetoes Violence	115
An Exit or an Exodus	117
Light of the World: A New Year Reflection	123
Little Man with a Melted Heart	125
Love Measures	127
The Family Framed	128
Cold Lips: Warm Love	130
New Hearts?	131
No Close-fistedness to a Buddha	133
No Longer Strangers	135
Overflow of the Altered Heart	137
Paul and Prosperity Preaching	139
Pauline Atonement Theology – Not Mine	141
Please, No Garlands Around My Neck	142
The World Is Where You Sit	144
Prayer, Buddha, and Jesus	146
In Gratitude to Buddhism	148
Running on Empty	148
Empty and Free (2006)	149
Prayers for Healing and Puzzlement	150
"I Do"	152
Roots and the River: Do Not Fear	154
(A Bit Of Buddhist Perspective)	155
Seeds of Justice and the Powers That Be	157

The Shona and the Seventh Year 159
Sinister Canopy of Nationalism 160
Then I Saw Her Face: Facades of Faith in the U.S. 161
Taming the Tongue 166
Teach Me to Pray, Dad 168
The Beginning of Strife 173
The Foul Beneath Our Feet 175
The Narrow Path of Love 177
The News Is Not Good 179
The Way 180
The Waiting Is Killing Me 182
Formative Guilt 183
To Be Saved or Salvaged? 187
Life Would Die on Her Lips 188
What Do I Lack? 190
What Is Your Life? 192
Who Is the Judge? 194
Why Worry? A Twinkle of Eternity 195
A Twinkle of Eternity 196
Wisdom in Foolishness 197
Women and Men of God 198
Epilogue: July 13, 2017 199

Acknowledgements

Perhaps I should change, but she has no expectation that I will. I suspect I will always be driven to wrestle with questions and uncertainties that my wife does not feel compelled to answer. Joan does not attempt to referee, blow any whistles, or stop the match. She waits for me, accepts me, and affirms the journey. Her faithfulness is freeing; so, I write. Thanks, Joan. I love you.

There are men in my life who for decades have shared with me the deepest dimensions of love. We have spent countless hours together reading and discussing books, opening our lives to each other, offering support, and calling for accountability. They have read and commented upon many of the writings in this text. I have been the beneficiary of their wisdom and prayers. There is an African proverb that states, "I am, because we are; we are because I am." While these brothers may not concur with everything in this book, much of who I am is a product of their companionship. To my brothers Dave and Jim Leaman, Rev. Jeff Lampl, and James Warren: I hope you like who I am becoming.

Twenty-seven years ago I received my Doctorate of Ministry to Marriage and Family from Eastern Baptist Theological Seminary, now Palmer Seminary. Doctors Carol and Peter Schreck were my professors for several courses. Following the three-year program Carol and I continued to meet several times a year, and in the sanctuary of her care I have bared my soul - wondered, wept, and laughed. It is only because of her encouragement that this book came to fruition. I am deeply grateful.

I close my acknowledgments with a sincere thanks to James Warren for the time he spent editing these writings and producing a work fit for publication. This was more than a random act of kindness. It was an enduring commitment to a lengthy and wearisome process, for the sake of a fifty-year friendship. May I be so fortunate to walk the path with him for many years to come.

In Love That Leads To Hope
Rev. Dr. Melvin I. Leaman

Introduction

These reflections were written with the sole intention of being honest with God in the moment. Morsels of comfort will be served, but other helpings may upset the stomach. Some will bring solace; some will disturb the silence. A number of them are inspirational as well as exegetical and informational, but most of the writings are personal responses to the scripture at hand. Here, the reader will be privy to the impermanent fluctuations of both faith and doubt, deep love for the Divine and disturbing feelings of distain. A quick scan of the table of contents previews the wide range of topics that will be addressed; essentially, a diary of one pilgrim's spiritual journey. It will be most meaningful for those who have experienced an impassioned hope to hold on to the faith that has filled them, as well as the familial expectations that have formed them. That is their Jerusalem; their fortification and sanctuary. Yet, the call to Alexandria, that foreign land of different perceptions and interpretations, constantly rings in their ears. As luring as the Sirens of Faiakes, this song stirs them to doubt the firm foundations on which they stand. To step into unchartered waters, and drift ever closer to new territories of faith that are as disconcerting as they are compelling. As the title of one chapter in this book puts it: is it an exit or an *exodus*? If you would like to pack your bags and take the trek with me, it may be a rewarding adventure.

You should know what brings me to this point of pen in hand: faith and doubt. From my formative years in the Mennonite tradition, through my adult career in the United Methodist ministry, faith and doubt have followed in tandem. I have loved and hated them equally; for whether promising or perplexing, both have birthed new understandings of self, life, and God. Eighteen years ago I left the pastorate because too many doubts plagued my soul. I began to feel dishonest when I stepped behind the pulpit, prayed by hospital beds, or eulogized at gravesides. At sixty-six years of age, I would like to feel more stability, standing firmly on something or someone. Yet there are still times when my foundations shake, and my toes bite down, struggling for purchase in the wave drenched sands, receding with the tide. While it may appear that I sometimes write with irreverent hubris, the audacious style is cushioned by what I hope is sincere humility. I am more pained than proud of this phase in my spiritual sojourn. There have been times when it has felt scary. The lapse in time between compilation and publication of these thoughts is explained by the fear of revealing myself to, and disappointing, those who experience me as a man of faith; while at the same time fearing lest the doubts expressed herein be a hindrance to sensitive readers. I finally concluded, however, that despite my hesitations my voice should be heard.

Peter Rollins, in his book *Insurrection* makes the following assertion: "While various religious systems provide a place for this painful experience of unknowing (as a test, as something to endure, or something to overcome), in Christianity when one is crushed by a deep, existential loss of certainty, one finds oneself in Christ." Yet my future in faith remains tenuous. I'm not sure what I am finding. The voice within queries: "Mel, why are you writing when so much remains in limbo? People like answers, Mel. They like authors who have been through the fire and pulled themselves together. But you . . . your thoughts are far from groomed, and your garments are not tucked. Wait until you look a bit more presentable. *Then* write."

I hear that voice, but in response I wonder, "Why did we have to wait until Mother Teresa died to be privy to her struggles to maintain faith? Honest to God, isn't there anyone else out there who shares my experiences of faith and doubt, who honors both and denies neither? Isn't there a kind of integrity that cannot be captured by retrospective, calm reflection after the battle, but drives the desperate scribblings of the one in the foxhole? I wrote these reflections from the foxhole. I appreciate Richard Rhor's recent comments regarding the collaboration of doubt and faith:

> "The movement through unknowing is necessary in all encounters, relationships, or intellectual breakthroughs, not just with the Divine. Human faith and religious faith are much the same except in their object or goal. What set us on the wrong path was making the object of religious faith 'ideas' or doctrines instead of a person. . . Faith is more how to believe than what to believe." (*Daily Devotions*, July, 18, 2017)

My foxhole scribblings are laid out before you: some full of faith, others fighting to keep it. Following years of struggle to find meaning in the discipline of daily devotions, I eventually let the practice die. One can't keep kicking a dead horse. And I assumed that beast of burden was not going to live again. But I was wrong. Determined to draw closer to God in some form or fashion, I decided to read only the verses in Sojourners Magazine's daily "Verse and Voice" – only the *verse*, not the accompanying commentary. I pondered the verses each day, and began to write. Those verses created the framework for the reflections addressed herein. These entries commenced with Advent 2010, and continued through January 2012. I did not start this project bent on writing for the sake of publication. Only recently, at the encouragement of my mentor, did I decide to compile them, eventuating in the book you hold. The format is an alphabetical listing by title of the various entries with the corresponding verse. Most of the entries are not dated, and most of the closing prayers are late additions to the readings, contributing, hopefully, to a more devotional style. They are short, simple, and heart-felt. On occasion, the prayer will be followed with a postscript.

These reflections in prose and poetry were written at different times over the past twelve years. They will give the interested reader the opportunity to know more about the family and religious influences that have formed me. Some of them are very brief, and others up to three or four pages in length. A few have been published.

As I repeat in a later entry, in his book *Wishful Thinking*, Frederick Buechner dares to say: "Doubt can be the ants in the pants of faith." I pray that he is right. Hopefully, *Honest With God: Reflections On Faith And Doubt* will encourage you to live with integrity amidst both faith and doubt.

A Bigger Brain or a Different Being?

[God] shall judge between many peoples, and shall arbitrate between strong nations far away; they shall beat their swords into plowshares, and their spears into pruning-hooks; nation shall not lift up sword against nation, neither shall they learn war anymore. *Micah 4:3*

Hope's torch sometimes casts the shadow of apocalyptic scenarios; but it also lights the way to a promising future. This is true within many religions, not just the Judeo-Christian tradition, where the dawn of a new age lies on the other side of apocalyptic doom and gloom. Humanity cannot accept that the imperfect and often painful experience of daily life – not to mention catastrophic apocalypse – is all there is. We join in the corporate cry, "But this can't be." And imagination summons a better future. Is this religious imagination a response to divine revelation? Or is it a deluded denial of a purposeless life that fades into the shadow of nothingness? Does it matter that we cannot prove either state of affairs to be the final one?

The truth is that human beings cannot help but hope. The Judeo-Christian creation story paints a paradise where the "lion will lie down with the lamb." Yet the real world of the author of that text would have been vicious. It would have been a place where predators shared the daily ritual of tearing their prey to shreds. The ruthlessness of survival haunted the ancient mind. They dreamed of a new dawn in history, when even the carnivores lost their lust for blood, and all of life found refuge in an idyllic paradise of peace. I suspect they sought to avoid pegging the violence of their world on the Creator. God was good. God was great. How then could such savagery happen?

The conclusion drawn by the Hebrew authors was that we did it to ourselves. The Genesis story implies that human *sin* put the taste for blood in the lion's mouth. The biblical authors dreamed of a day when humanity could put down their swords, melt them into pruning hooks, and prepare the way for the Messiah. We learned in Sunday School that heaven would be the only place such peace could happen. Whether or not we cherish beliefs in heaven and creation, the phenomenon of hope is worth considering. We know of no other mammal that consciously laments the viciousness of the present world and longs for a future paradise. Is that a matter of a bigger brain, or an entirely different order of being, of spirit? If we are creatures who spring from the Creator's heart, could the mere fact that peoples from all over the world hold on to hope suggest that hope is worth holding onto? I'll let God be the judge of that, but I do know this: I am a better person when hope fashions my heart.

> *O God, grant that the flicker of hope will light my way. May it be as real as the darkness. Let heaven happen now, and in all the "thens" to come. Amen.*

A Black Jesus

And suddenly there was with the angel a multitude of the heavenly host, praising God and saying, 'Glory to God in the highest heaven, and on earth peace among those whom [the Lord] favors. Luke 2:13-14

Is Barak Obama the first black President, or is he the first president who is black? That question has been a matter of significant debate for African Americans. Those who would call him the first black President would point to policies that address specific issues related to black people, while those claiming that Obama is merely a president who happens to be black will say that he is, like so many others, a politician who is owned by and caters to systems of white privilege and power.

James Cone contends in his book, *God of the Oppressed*, that if you do not know that Jesus is black, then you do not know Jesus. He is referring not to a matter of skin color, but the spirit that lives within. We give credence to the image of God within each of us, which gives every one of us the dignity of Divine inheritance, yet we create societies that demean the poor in personhood and pocketbook. The Incarnate God is black because this One knows the suffering of the poor. He too felt the whip of Roman oppression.

When Cone was writing, the Civil Rights era was in full swing as a direct consequence of people who believed in God's preferential treatment of the poor, the marginalized, and the disenfranchised. Jesus did not hob-knob with the rich and righteous, but with the destitute and undeserving. Jesus knew what it was like to live on the other side of the tracks. His promise was for the projects! There is a stroke of scandalous genius in Luke's painting of a nativity scene where the good news story of a silent night breaks before a small group of poor shepherds who were scorned by the blessed elite. Luke's nativity story was libelous. In chapter one he has the audacity to put the language of victory and power in the mouths of two poor, praying saints: Mary and Zechariah. Chapter two portrays a babe born under the oppressive arm of Caesar who will challenge that rule and win. While contextualized within the framework of the Roman subjugation of the Jews, the story breathes whispers and rumors of white privilege and racism today. How would wealthy, white U.S. citizens have heard prophetic announcements of the birth and future accomplishments of Martin Luther King, Jr., coming from the mouths of marginalized black parents? This news would not have sounded like Gospel, like "good news." On the contrary, it would have struck fear in the hearts of many hearers, because an entire social structure was about to be threatened.

The spirit of the black Jesus is portrayed in a parable told by the philosopher, John Rawls. It is usually referred to as "the veil of ignorance." In brief, a small group of people are arguing over the establishment of a fair and just society. The leader eventually grants them the opportunity to create their own society with one stipulation: they must shape it without any foreknowledge or planning of the position each of them would hold within the new society. It will be created under a "veil of ignorance." No one will know in which economic strata of society s/he is destined to live. The framers of the constitution for this brotherhood would enter the halls of congress with nagging questions: "What if I am one of the poor? How will I be protected, if not preferred and favored, by the laws of the land?" Out of this personal angst, a fair and just society would be possible.

Now, that's a pretty picture for the poor shepherds of any time. That's the story of God's love, incarnate – the earthy side of Jesus. In the end, to favor the poor is to favor all. Good news! The glory of God in the highest heaven is most radiant when peace and justice reigns for the lowly of the earth. Joy to the world!

> *Dear Jesus, I pray for both the aspiration and audacity to labor for the kind of justice that looks like joy to the whole world. Do not allow me to be whisked away by the gentle breezes of my pampered socio-economic reality. Push me beyond the boundaries of my experience, so that the commitments of my time, talent, and treasure bring good news to those who would otherwise remain strangers. Amen.*

Postscript
Conditioned by Racism and Called to Reconciliation (2009)

As I turned into the CVS pharmacy lot, I saw three African Americans standing by a car in the corner. The stereotype amused me: black guys hanging out together can't be a good thing. There was no genuine suspicion or fear on my part. After all, this wasn't downtown Philadelphia. I figured they were Lincoln University students. And sure enough, one of them was a newcomer to my Introduction to Religion class.

My faded, red '93 Escort remained unnoticed as I parked it a few spaces from the corner. Pondering how to approach starting a conversation with these young men, I closed the door to my car and called out in a joking manner, "Hey, you guys, don't you know you're not supposed to be loitering around here!" As I stepped towards them, one of the young men immediately began to defend their presence: "Ah, man, we're not doing anything. We're just waiting for a friend to get some things at the pharmacy."

I have a good rapport with my students, so by the time I was close enough for Shawn to recognize me, he reached out his hand: "Hey, Dr. Leaman. What's happening?" He jovially informed his friends that I was one of his professors. Feeling very uncomfortable for initially putting them on the defensive, I foolishly added, "I thought I might get you on that one." They laughed. We talked.

I walked into the store completely disenchanted by my lack of sensitivity. I just didn't expect to see three strapping young black men kowtow to some little, balding white guy; or did I? Why in the world did I *even jokingly* accuse them of being up to no good and loitering? Who or what in my world told me that it was appropriate to make that comment to a group of African American young men? In an instant, these guys were falling all over themselves apologizing for being somewhere they had every right to be. I had momentarily emasculated the very people I was attempting to empower in my classroom. The question that some of my colleagues pose raced through my mind: Should a white guy teach in a black institution of higher learning? How did I succumb to the inherent power of my color? Those students should have been indignant: "How dare some white guy under the pretense of friendship put us in this position!" As I pulled away from the scene I felt even more saddened by their apparent absence of anger.

Repentance is much more than saying the words "I'm sorry." It is the action of making an "about face." Sincere repentance is a step towards reconciliation, a response to the cry for renewal of relationship. Dumbfounded by Jesus' demonstrative gesture to break down prejudice and classism, Zacchaeus exemplified an active repentance by pledging to pay back four-fold those whom he defrauded (Luke 19:1-10). Moreover, he knew this would require a *face-to-face* encounter. He knew that true repentance was much more interpersonal than a quick confession to God. The responsibility to mend the damage – even unacknowledged damage – rests upon the offender, the powerful, and the privileged.

When Shawn came to class the next day I asked to speak with him privately, and our conversation went like this:

"Shawn, I really need to apologize for what I said the other day in the parking lot."

"Oh, no Dr. Leaman it's ok. It was nothing."

"No Shawn, it was something. You guys have to kowtow enough to white men like me. I didn't like the way it must have made you feel. I should not have said those things and I apologize." (I considered that asking Shawn to forgive me would have been more about my need than his. It might have put him on the defensive, and once again I would have been in control. I chose instead simply to apologize.)

"Yeah. Ok, Dr. Leaman, I know what you mean." Our closing handshake led to a quick embrace.

Prior to the termination of our time together, I asked Shawn for the names and phone numbers of the other two students. I did not know them. Later that day, I had the chance to apologize to one of them personally. I called the other young man. In retrospect, I was distressed by my misuse of power as a professor and privileged white man. Once the words came out of my mouth, their response was scripted by centuries of accommodation. Even if they felt angry, they had to swallow it and sheepishly defend themselves, like so many times before. Perhaps that is what caught me off guard and revealed the depth of my offense: the fact that they so quickly, and without thinking, submitted to my stereotypical interrogation. These young men had been conditioned to deny their dignity. I am still conditioned to use my privilege. Sadly, we are both still enslaved.

No one, on occasions like this, captures my inner disquiet more profoundly than the Apostle Paul: "O wretched man that I am, who can deliver me from this body of death" (Romans 7:24). Despite a sincere desire to quell my privileges and prejudices, their remnants still fester deep within my soul. When they show themselves they magnify differences, intensify fears, and minimize our shared experiences of being human. They lead to a separatist's hell and a relational death. How do I destroy these imprints on the brain with all their personal and social ramifications: she's pretty smart for a black girl; he's a real compliment to his race; once you go black you never come back; black people are lazy; black people pull the moral standards of our nation down; black men are violent. . . . The list could go on.

Paul concludes, "the law of the Spirit of life in Christ Jesus has set me free from the law of sin and death" (Romans 8:2). He and I both take Jesus seriously when Jesus says, "The truth shall set you free" (John 8:32). The truth about me is that my efforts to reach beyond the confines of racism are inevitably complicit with the personal and systemic privilege of my whiteness.

I try to live confessionally before God, and with my African American brothers and sisters. We are both victims of systemic principalities and powers that propagate sin and separation. We both need to name these powers and know how they formed us. These systems have warped our perceptions of self and each other. When I showed this article to an African American colleague who has co-published with me, he concurred with my conviction of our mutual loss of right perceptions. He also expressed concern regarding the degree to which African Americans have accepted a position of victimization, and therefore permitted the "Euro" to define them and their behavior. He suggested that in many cases, sadly enough, the oppressed succumb to the behavioral expectations of the oppressor.

I appreciated his willingness to consider the part that African Americans may play in the relational mix. On the other hand, he aired deep frustration over the fact that white people have turned deaf ears to the black story: "Mel, I can talk to white people for hours and they will conclude that I am simply an angry black man who doesn't realize he is the problem." Black people are tired of telling their stories. Although my friend does not completely agree with me, I believe the impetus for reconciliation begins with white men and women. It commences with a passion for a pure heart: *Search me, O God, and see if there be any wicked way in me* (Psalm 139:23-24). It is followed by confession and repentance for personal and corporate sin. My colleague noted that while forgiveness can be an individual act, *reconciliation* requires the determination of both parties to no longer allow the offense to define the relationship or permit it to be used as a weapon against the other. Therefore, he was unwilling to assign the initiative for reconciliation exclusively to one side of the color line or the other.

Repentance necessitates relationship. Christian white people for centuries have vigorously attempted to distance themselves from their black brothers and sisters; it is now imperative that with equal vigor we take the initiative to pursue meaningful and healing relationships. Jesus said: "So if you are offering your gift at the altar, and there remember that your brother has something against you, leave your gift there before the altar and go; first to be reconciled with your brother" (Matthew 5:23-24). However, even when taking this seemingly God-honoring step towards reconciliation, white people must continually seek the truth as to whether they are initiating the relationship primarily as a means of appeasing personal guilt, or whether they harbor a genuine desire for ongoing relational give-and-take.

Early in our relationship my colleague bluntly told me, "I don't know if I can trust you because you're white." A year or so later, after we established a friendship, he reflected upon that statement and added: "I decided to take the risk because I chose to believe that this white man might be more like me than different from me, and that we need each other to be fully human, fully alive."

Yes, we have both been conditioned by the racism of the past, but in the kingdom of Christ we are called now to share the abundant life of reconciliation that will be our future. Shawn and his friends long for that kind of kingdom. So do I.

A Burning Love

For you were called to freedom, brothers and sisters; only do not use your freedom as an opportunity for self-indulgence, but through love become slaves to one another. For the whole law is summed up in a single commandment, 'You shall love your neighbor as yourself.' If, however, you bite and devour one another, take care that you are not consumed by one another. Galatians 5:13-15

The fire of my freedom can consume my brother. He becomes "the other." The fruits of the spirit mentioned only a few verses later in Galatians, are left to rot in the tree when the desire to be right trumps the desire for right relationship. When competition rages, the contestants are bound by a chain of entitlements and resentments. Both the offended and the offender are chained to their separate but equally demeaning dungeons of distain. They paint self-indulgent pictures on their prison walls showing scenes of the other's culpability. Here is gnashing and grinding of teeth that tear the soul, for one cannot cherish a self that scorns the other. Each forgets – he *is* the other. The two rivals are one in their obsessive drive to devalue each other, as well as in their need to be affirmed. It is a costly joust! Freedom is held captive to the fear of losing face. It is captive to the feud, and to the thin façade of piety that thinly disguises the flesh of an uncircumcised heart.

In these times, when the twain shall never meet, even under the enslaving gavel of legality, let us hope they can yet be set free beneath the unfurled banner of love.

O Consuming Fire, unfurl your banner above me. Flag any part that strays from your burning love. When ego covets the cry of victory at the cost of relational intimacy, keep my eyes upon your cross. When the flashing sword invigorates me and the taste of vengeance slavers my mouth, call to my remembrance that I am swallowing seeds of death. When I should be so stubborn as to seek the win that leads to loss, humble my heart, heal my woundedness, less I should forget Thine own. Amen.

A Choice and A Curse

I call heaven and earth to witness against you today that I have set before you life and death, blessings and curses. Choose life so that you and your descendants may live.
Deuteronomy 30:19

Just a few minutes ago, on my drive home, I was visited again by an unwelcomed thought. Peering through the front window of my Civic into the vast, open sky before me, it flashed across my mind: "I'm fooling myself; there is no God up there, down, over, under or anywhere." I despise the fact that my head so frequently challenges my heart. It is with loathing that I pound-out on this keyboard the reality of this dilemma; would that such doubts could be "as far as the East is from the West." Yet, rarely does a day pass without doubt. Too afraid to affirm the atheist wandering through the back woods of my mind, I silence his taunts with scripture, personal stories of transformative faith, and family traditions that have formed me. The atheist fades into the forest with haunting accusations of cowardliness. We both know he will be back. I simply cannot comprehend how it has come to be that despite six decades of life-giving blessings, I am cursed with constant thoughts about the death of God. How in the world can this conflicted soul find assurance that my "descendants may (will) live" – let alone love the God I question?

The atheist's appeal is strong, yet I can hardly fathom living without God. Leaving one's faith is much more than casting aside creeds that no longer nourish the soul. It is the loss of meaningful rituals that have formed the imagination since childhood. Just the thought of never praying with my grandchildren because I no longer believe in God paralyzes me with grief. Will I never pause for even a brief prayer before a meal? Must I brush away all those memories of Mom and Dad praying with me as just so much dust collected on a shelf? Am I to conclude that family time and prayers with my own children were worthless petitions to an imaginary deity? How do I instill in my grandchildren a sense of gratitude for the handiwork of creation, when I have left the belief in a Creator behind? How do I talk about hope if I conclude that what they can conjure within themselves is the only hope they have? Questions upon questions. Doubt conjured from depths I fear to ponder.

> *O God, just how far is the East from the West? Thoughts that affirm a love for you as well as those of choosing to live in a world without you have been swirling in my mind for fifteen years and more. I do not glory in the gap between us. Call your witnesses against me, threaten me with death, strip the hope of the eternal from my soul and I still cannot quell the questions. If belief is simply a matter of the will, there are times when I have not the will to believe. Yet, I long to believe in a love that outlives the confines of time itself. All I can say is that distance does not make the heart grow fonder. All I can pray is "Dear God, do what I cannot." Amen.*

A New Twist on What We Treasure

Do not store up for yourselves treasures on earth, where moth and rust consume and where thieves break in and steal; but store up for you treasures in heaven, where neither moth nor rust consumes and where thieves do not break in and steal. For where your treasure is, there your heart will be also. Matthew 6:19-21

What captures heaven's heart? "And You have made him/her a little lower than the angels" (Psalm 8:5). *You and I* are the delight of the Creator. God's hope for us is not a deep-pocket of prosperity, but a healthy pursuit of loving relationship with one another. "Love is the more excellent way" for both friend and foe. The glory of God is not a heavy-handed authority or a halo-headed Jesus. If "God is love," then as Justo L. Gonzalez puts it: "God is being-for-others." It is this being-for-others that is reflected most fully in the life, death, and resurrection of Jesus. Inasmuch as you and I treat all others with the dignity of angels unawares, particularly the poor, the oppressed, and the marginalized, we are living examples of for-otherness, and present an image of the Divine Incarnate to the world.

O Living One who has instilled within our being the truth of that which we need cherish, protect us from clinging to personal ownership and closing our hands to the poor, salvage us from the clutter of life that leads to the junkyards of personal despair and communal languish, and empower us with the vision to see beyond self-servitude. Amen

A Strange Messiah

Shower, O heavens, from above, and let the skies rain down righteousness; let the earth open, that salvation may spring up, and let it cause righteousness to sprout up also; I the Lord have created it. Isaiah 45:8

Israel was in exile. No longer secure in the Promised Land, they lamented their captivity and God's apparent abandonment of them. Yet their prophets, like Isaiah, would not permit them to sink into total despair. Surely, the prophets proclaimed, as God delivered his children from enslavement in Egypt, God would send a Messiah ("Anointed One" in Hebrew) to free them from bondage in Babylon. Still whirling from the shock that God would allow this tragedy to happen to his Chosen People, the Israelites tearfully hung their harps on the willows by the riverside, wept, and waited for their redemption (Psalm 137:2). There just *had* to be a Moses standing in the wings, ready to sweep across the stage for another dramatic rescue. The curtain could not fall at the close of the final act with Israel still languishing in captivity. This story had been scripted by the Deity. The playwright had promised peace in the homeland; not terror within their captors' walls.

They did not hope in vain. There were more pages to be turned in their epic drama of salvation history. Suddenly, an unexpected player appears front and center. He is not a Moses. If fact, he isn't even one of the Israelites' own. This man is a *foreigner* sent by God. "For the sake of Israel my chosen…I will strengthen you, though you have not acknowledged me, so that from the rising of the sun to the place of its setting people may know there is none beside me. I am the Lord, there is no other" (Isaiah 45:4-6). The only person in the Hebrew Scriptures who is specifically given the title of Messiah – the Lord's anointed – will be a foreign king. *Cyrus*, king of Persia, will swoop down upon the Babylonians, defeat them, and eventually declare that the children of Israel may march back to Zion. God's righteousness pours from the heavens through the hands of a stranger.

Perhaps this Advent I should look for God in faces of the unfamiliar.

O God of the stranger's way, humble me enough to see your face in her countenance and hear your wisdom in his words. Amen.

Baptism of Love

[John the baptizer] proclaimed, 'The one who is more powerful than I is coming after me; I am not worthy to stoop down and untie the thong of his sandals. I have baptized you with water; but he will baptize you with the Holy Spirit.
Mark 1:7-8

How did John know anything about the Holy Spirit? Pentecost was post-crucifixion, plus fifty days. If his utterance was prophetic it could not have been understood or even imagined by John's audience. Is this the declaration of a redactor, privileged with hindsight? After all, the author is writing some thirty years after Jesus' resurrection, and his readers will already have witnessed the Spirit of Pentecost and the power of Jesus.

Just how did Jesus put power in its proper place? If we jump to the Gospel of John, we will see that while John the Baptist could only point the way to God through repentance from the sin that has estranged the people from an angry God, Jesus had the power to lay them securely in the lap of a loving Father. The Baptizer's guilt-laden message might have scared a few into the kingdom, but Jesus' call to be the children of God has a more intimate flavor. *There is no fear in love* (I John 4:18). Scholars conclude that the closest interpretation for the word power in Mark's text is *empowerment*. The life, death, and resurrection of Jesus enables believers to see themselves and God in a new light. The forceful and ultimately condemning power of the law is weakened by the empowering love that captures the longing of every heart.

Every child wants to know warmth and acceptance. Children make mistakes by both volition and ignorance, and their repentance is motivated by fear of rejection. Jesus is that face of forgiveness that frees us from the dread of condemnation. The love of God Incarnate, Jesus, looks down from heaven, is hung high on a cross, and stands victorious beside an empty tomb. We find our story in his story. Neither our deeds nor our death have the final word. Jesus draws us unto himself. Our delight in that love gives birth to a new spirit of desire to walk in the light of God's love. We experience the joy of a cherished child. We never feel worthy of that kind of acceptance: a lowly stoop in gratitude is the best we can do. As John states: "But to all who received him, who believed in his name, he gave power to become the children of God" (St. John 1:12).

> *Dear Jesus, release me from fear. When I doubt God's love and wallow in condemnation, let me see your face; let me hear your words; let me taste and see that the Lord is good. Amen.*

Postscript
Let's Drink to That! (2006)

"Pour another cold one for my friend," Jesus said, as he set a mug on the counter. "Give him some from that new skin. This man has so much hardship hanging around his neck, he needs a few hits to ease him up a bit. Believe me, I know what it takes to soothe a man's soul."

Others gathered around the bar raised their cups toward Heaven. They cheered the generosity of this man who often lit up the scene with a grin that seemed to say: "Gentlemen, God forbid I should not show you a good time!" Love and laughter seemed to pour out of him. Jesus was about a joy that went much deeper than the accusation of being a juiced-up "wine-bibber." Bar room brawls were quelled to a whisper as he unflinchingly stood between fist-slinging opponents. It was not merely rumor that Jesus had taken blows to the jaw meant for a man behind him. He had this quiet, confident way about him that for some reason mellowed the macho in every man. Between the loud "you belong with us" bellowing, and the "good buddy" pats on the back, the guys at the bar sensed that sitting in the same room with Jesus was strangely serendipitous (although they wouldn't have said it like that). Maybe the Magdalenes who slithered their contoured bodies into darkened side rooms, resonated more closely with these feelings of warmth. Sidling up to the bar was all about warmth. Here people listened to your story. They accepted you. No one was interested in removing logs from the other's sore eyes.

Did not Jesus love the sinner on the bar stool as much as the one in the synagogue? Jesus resisted saintly piety, but wherever true confessions were told he inspired the creation of a new heart. He marked the beginning of his ministry with a metaphor that has new wine fermenting, then oozing out through old seams, and finally bursting the sides of wineskins that could not possibly contain the freshness. These "spirits" truly were for what ails you! His life was not about cold looks and long faces. It was about warmth and belonging. It was about letting go and laughing 'til the cows came home.

They did come home. It wasn't a furrowed brow but a smiling face that summoned them. There was no question in Jesus' mind about what it took to set people free: just break out the new wine! Look again and you'll see him cracking jokes in Cana with the other wedding guests, sharing a cup of wine in the house of Zacchaeus, or pouring a nightcap for Nicodemus. Listen to his stories. How many party parables can one man conjure? The prodigal comes home, so kill the fatted calf and fill the table with the finest foods. Host a banquet for friends and if they snub the invitation, bring in the bums off the cold streets sipping Boone's Farm. They'll get a taste of the good stuff at Jesus' table! If you think you deserve the best seat at the next party you better set your bottom down somewhere else because in this house "the first shall be last and the last shall be first." All kinds of people came home to Jesus. He never pondered, "What would Jesus do?" Rather, he asked, "What does the face of love look like?" He focused upon the last, the least, the lost, and the lonely. The wine was flowing, and they found life in his presence.

It was time to say farewell. The stools were scooted up at the bar in the company of his closest friends.

"This is my body you eat. This is my blood you drink. Do this in remembrance of me." His disciples ate and drank in silent solidarity. Then came Calvary. Could it be that the human face of pain on the cross disguised the face of a deity who died laughing? By the third day the roar of his laughter resounded to a loud climax that shattered all fear. The stone rolled away, and the world would never be the same.

Today the eucharistic fellowship remembers that event with a respectful somberness. Yet how can we share in thanksgiving without a smile? Dare we imagine Jesus in our presence tipping the chalice skyward and with an endearing laugh saying, "Pour another cold one for my friends"? And with grinning faces and grateful hearts we lift our cups towards the heavens and cry out, like Luther, "Blood (love) of Christ inebriate me!" Jesus was about new wine. Jesus was about joy. Let's drink to that!

Being Still: Is God Safe?

Be still and know that I am God. Psalm 46:10

I am learning to be still. Recently, however, my consolation has been practicing the Buddha's call to stay in the moment and to live in the peace that all things pass. That is different than the Apostle Paul's "peace that passes all understanding." The former peace comes from within, but the latter peace is a gift from God. I struggle to maintain a deep assurance that God is somehow in control of my life, and the life of the global village.

The Hebrew Scriptures sometimes promoted the theological perspective that everything that happened was not only ordained by the Almighty, but fashioned or fated by Him. Therefore, when floods came, when victims fell to war or plague, when barren women brought forth children – all these could be attributed to God. The Hebrews simply trusted that the best approach to life was to let God be God.

I choose not to be so trusting. For this kind of trust actually diminishes God to the level of earthly happenings. Many would differ with me and contend that letting God be God is an acknowledgement of humility, and the exultation God deserves. After all, I am not God, and I don't know. Perhaps my sinful, shaking hand reaches with Eve's to pick of that tree whose fruit damns me to knowing too much. Maybe I am the one with the control issues, not God.

> *Dear God, I confess that all the suffering in the world causes me to question why we were created and whether or not you are, and if you are, in control. I'm not convinced that it is safe to "be still," yet I feel equally insecure in a belief that you are of my own making. Sometimes, I think I would be happier if I did not have to think about you. In my stillness, the silence screams. It is not, O God, that I long to do my own thing and live a life of self-serving debauchery, but it is rather that I grow so weary of trying to defend you. Amen.*

Postscript
Get Me to the Quiet (2010)

Get me to the quiet ever so quick
Where the sap runs slow
And the trees hang thick
The stream is low
And the trickles sound
No one else dare be around.

Rest my head where I once hid
And my heart is hushed
By the katydid
But the hind is flushed
Its lair revealed
Now, leaps the stream to open field.
I settled there on grassy knoll

And with a heavy sigh
Released my soul
From the haunting why
Of the daily bread
This suffering world is too often fed.

Blaming and Scapegoating the Poor

The poor are disliked even by their neighbors, but the rich have many friends. Proverbs 14:20

The Judeo-Christian Scriptures are imbued with this truism. Authors of the Bible repeatedly stand on the soapbox of justice proclaiming the favor of God upon the poor, and spewing forth disapproval of those who selfishly side with the rich. Sometimes we *unknowingly* befriend the wealthy. A few days ago, one of my brothers – a very generous person to those in need – was lamenting the state of our economy, and blaming much of our present dilemma on the dishonesty of people who take advantage of the welfare programs our government offers. I suggested that many more millions of dollars are lost to the manipulation of loopholes and lack of ethics in the business practices of the rich. Our disagreement might have been settled by statistics, but neither of us were armed with any, so we each went our way convinced that our own conviction was the truth.

Regardless of who might have had the statistics on his side, had we been able to produce them, we know that it is much easier to blame those who cannot defend themselves than those who hold the wealth and power of the system. Of course, it must be admitted that the poor will sometimes point the finger at the rich as a means of escaping their own responsibilities. As Rene Girard posits, societies in conflict rally around a scapegoat. The poor have their own scapegoats; but in the larger society, the typical scapegoat is the voiceless poor, and they become society's sacrificial victim. Opposing factions within society point their fingers at the scapegoat, discovering unity over-against a common enemy. So once again a sense of community is restored, and the factions get along – for a while. So powerful is this "ritual," that the scapegoat takes on an almost sacred role. It becomes necessary for unity.

> *God, who holds all peoples in Her care, keep us from being so swaddled by our own beneficence that we forget to reach out to others of less fortune. As you were in Jesus, may we be the voice of the victim rather than the keepers of the system. Amen.*

Buy Me Some Poverty

Listen, my beloved brothers and sisters. Has not God chosen the poor in the world to be rich in faith and to be heirs of the kingdom that [God] has promised to those who love [the Lord]? James 2:5

Sometimes I wish I were "the poor." At the risk of romanticizing the poor and glorifying poverty, they really do seem to have preferred status in the Kingdom of God. It's almost as if they could stand before God in judgment with an *I Was Poor* placard on their chest, and Jesus would immediately intervene with "Hey, I got your back," and usher them to the V.I.P. section. There they would be seated by the smiling, angelic hostess and rightly served a gin and tonic.

What is it with these poor people? What do they have in their poverty that I lack in my wealth? Could it be that they have faith enough to say "let God be God" in this life, while I fight to control not only the happenstance but even the holy? Are they filled with an abundance of joyful abandonment while my resistance leaves me empty and longing? Their strength rests in the weakness of their dependence, while my muscled independence leads to an atrophied soul. In the end, I guess the poor in spirit really are the richest people around. I'm going to borrow one of those placards – or maybe I should just love the Lord.

My confession this morning, God, is that I too often question the deep things of life and love from dawn to dusk. I don't like you or trust you enough to say, "let God be God." My poverty resides in pockets of fear about the future. I do not think that I have reconciled with my own death. I pray that someday, some morning I will be able to awaken with enough faith to smile at the mysteries. Amen.

Called and Clueless

This is my commandment, that you love one another as I have loved you. John 15:12

That's a pretty tough call to imitate. Let's see now, you handpicked a group of guys from assorted vocations, bearing various personal eccentricities, and dared to call them friends. You determined to bring this ragtag gang to some level of understanding of a mission that pushed the boundaries of personal and social wholeness. You put up with simplistic questions, childish behavior, and selfish betrayal; yet you loved them. Finally, they, like all the others around them, either ran away or stood clueless beneath the cross; yet you blessed them with an unconditional word of forgiveness. You closed your final hours on earth with the call to mirror the gospel in the global village.

> *Jesus, I sometimes stand clueless at the foot of the cross. Yet, your words and your ways have captured me. They look like life to me. Thank you. Amen.*

Postscript
Can I be a Man of God? (April 6, 2000)

He rose from his chair with tear-filled eyes, and an expression of deep gratitude and release glowing upon his countenance. Pulling a handkerchief from his back pocket he sniffled a few times.

"Mel, from the first time I met you, I knew you were a man of God." I acknowledged his comment with a sincere gesture of thanks, while my soul smacked with a sense of hypocrisy.

Me, "a man of God!" If you only knew, my brother, how much this so-called godly counselor questions his God. If you could only see the short spurts of half-believing prayer. If you could observe my present resistance to studying the very scriptures I quote so easily, would you so quickly render me such reverence?

Thus, with a sense of shame I told my spiritual director of my consternation regarding this perception with which others dignify me. Can it be that I am what I do not see? He asked me some questions to assist the sorting process:

Do you believe that you are offering hope rather than hurt? Yes.

Are you leading them into love? Yes.

Are you insincere in the midst of praying with your clients? No.

Do you purposely put yourself in a position of expressing faith you do not feel? No.

Are you seeing evidence of God using your ministry? Yes.

Do you hold a genuine compassion for your clients? Yes.

"Then," she said, "you are a man of God."

In that moment I sheepishly accepted the possibility. But now I ask another question: can I be a man of God if I am not a disciple of Jesus? In other words, if I now question Jesus as the incarnation of God, if I cannot affirm the claim that Jesus is the only way to God, if I do not chose to affirm creedal Christianity exclusively, if I contend that somehow, by God's mercy, those of other faiths may be part of the Kingdom of God, if I do not feel compelled to share Christ when conversing with people . . . and if, at the end of it all, Jesus *is* God, can I be a man of God without being a disciple of Jesus?"

Can A Non-Christian Abide in That Love?

As the [Lord] has loved me, so I have loved you; abide in my love. If you keep my commandments, you will abide in my love, just as I have kept my [Lord's] commandments and abide in [God's] love. I have said these things to you so that my joy may be in you, and that your joy may be complete. John 15:9-11

The story goes that Rabbi Hillel, a contemporary of Jesus, took the tease of his disciples and declared that he could not only quote the entire Torah, he could do so while standing on one foot. The back-and-forth badgering continued until the respected Rabbi finally lifted a foot and began to speak: "Love the Lord your God with all your heart, soul, and mind, and love your neighbor as yourself." That's all he said. A period of silence followed the profundity of his witness. After a long, pregnant pause, he continued, "When the disciple determines to love God and neighbor, he fulfills the entire Torah."

The letter of the law was considered a gift from God. To keep the law brought delight to the Creator and joy to the created. It was the path to living in right relationship with God and neighbor. The intent was *love*. We read in Psalm 19 how the people would sing, "We love Thy precepts, O God." In like manner, the Muslims consider sharia (Islamic) law to be the sacred path that leads to God's delight. The Arabic image of a watering hole springs to the Muslim's mind when they think of sharia. In a world where nourishment was limited to the serendipity of a desert oasis, the watering hole was a place of refreshment and great joy. The Quran witnessed to a merciful God who gave them this sacred guide to the right path.

Jesus could say that he didn't come to destroy the law, but to fulfill it, because the intent of every good law was an expression of love for God or neighbor. Could it be said that the Jew, the Christian, or anyone from any faith (or none) who loves God and neighbor, has the joy of Jesus abiding in his heart? Maybe, when the day comes that they see Jesus, these people who had never known the fullness of his love, will bow and confess that in some form or fashion they knew him all along. Their hearts will have finally found a home.

> *Dear God, may your mercy be as broad as your Son suggests. May there truly be sheep who are not of your fold. I do not think I can follow you, if this is not the case. Please open your gates of grace to those who hear your voice, but do not know your name. Amen.*

Can A Prisoner Be Free?

I therefore, the prisoner in the Lord, beg you to lead a life worthy of the calling to which you have been called, with all humility and gentleness, with patience, bearing with one another in love, making every effort to maintain the unity of the Spirit in the bond of peace. Ephesians 4:1-3

My immediate response to this reading centered upon the word "prisoner." What does it mean to be a prisoner of the Lord? The very phraseology sounds like an oxymoron. We read all those verses that speak about the freedom that comes with knowing Jesus: "he shall set you free indeed" (John 8:36; Galatians 5:1). How can a prisoner be *free*?

There is a significant part of me that celebrates my captivity to the will and way of Jesus Christ. I feel blessed with a better way to live in relationship with others. I see myself in the other at his worst and at her best, so I am able to be merciful and compassionate. Jesus forgives, and I am bound in freedom to do the same. I am free to confess my need to be salvaged; put back on track by the empowerment of the Holy Spirit. I can choose to be of the same mind as Jesus, who humbled himself and became an exemplary servant of personal wholeness and communal justice.

Contextually, this verse is Paul's plea to the church to live in peace and practice patience with one another. This goal needs to be in the forefront of our minds in every situation. We are called to this covenant of love. We are constrained, held captive, prisoners of this pact with God and others. And here, we couldn't be happier.

Lord over us, under us, beside us, and live through us, O God. Empower us and enslave us to your goodness, to that we may serve as effective witnesses to our world for love's sake. Keep us from petty bickering, jealousy, and majoring in minor matters that mean little to the kingdom of God come to earth. Help us to see beyond our truncated imaginations that distance ourselves from others and are stumbling blocks to those who may otherwise draw near to You. Amen.

Can't Face Those Demons Alone

Put on the whole armor of God, so that you may be able to stand against the wiles of the devil. For our struggle is not against enemies of blood and flesh, but against the rulers, against the authorities, against the cosmic powers of this present darkness, against the spiritual forces of evil in the heavenly places. Ephesians 6:11-12

I have never bought into the scenario of angels and demons engaging in cosmic battle for the allegiance of personal souls or global authority. The Apostle Paul had his own way of expressing a powerful truth. At the same time, however, I do not deny the insidious, addictive, and absolutely destructive nature of accumulated, communal sin. At a certain threshold human community can lose principles of morality and move into a morass of evil that engulfs them to the point where good people engage in horrendous activities, powerless to resist.

For me, this "present darkness… in the heavenly places" resides in my heart and head. While the expansive part of me loves goodness, there are times when evil is as close as my jugular vein – to participate in it feels life-giving. Its power is frightfully compelling. Despite the hope-filled words of the song that "just a little talk with Jesus makes it right," sometimes the only way to remain constant and steadfast is to tell another person about my struggle, and ask him or her to hold me accountable. It is vertiginously dangerous to stand alone on the edge of a precipice. I need a partner's hand to stop me from plunging into the abyss.

O God of Power, embrace us with loving arms that will not let us go. While we remain grateful for the wonderful freedom that you have granted us there are times when we simply are too weak to choose right. We need your Spirit to cling tightly to our collars. Otherwise, we fall. Whether the abyss be personal or systemic dehumanizing darkness, somehow stay our feet in the daylight of truth. Finally, give us such humility that we recognize and utilize the resources of energizing love that is ours in the brother or sister. Sometimes, it is so much easier to see your face in them, than it is to see your face alone. Many times, the face of the intimate friend is the only image that will salvage us from sin and save our future. Amen.

Postscript
A Tribute to a Friend and Mentor (Carol Schreck)

So deeply do we care for you that we are determined to share with you not only the gospel of God but also our own selves, because you have become very dear to us. 1 Thessalonians 2:8

The gift of love creates a hallowed place amidst the chaos of life, a place where the heart finds a harbor, where trust finds her temple, and honesty finds his home. It is not always a comfortable space, but it is a haven where your soul can rest in the blessed assurance that the other truly seeks your best welfare. Here the gospel of God, the good news of a greater love, transforms human dialogue into dimensions of holiness. Then, one-on-one, our world and our words are sacralized by the three-in-one, whose presence burns away any chaff surrounding kernels of truth hidden in our hearts for fear of exposure. Together we determine that the gospel of God will be the lamp that lightens our darkness, no matter how painful the rays of penetrating truth. We share ourselves in with care and covenantal integrity. Here we discover the depths of what it means to say, "You have become very dear to us." It is one thing to know the love of Jesus Christ and to pass it on, but it is quite another to share "our own selves." The latter is that narrow way for the few who dare to believe that, although the Creator has entrusted us as vessels of God's vernacular, these fragile, clay pots of self are not all they are cracked up to be. Consequently, we find hope and healing in the prayers and cares of the hearts of those who hold us dear. Thank you for creating that hallowed place amidst the chaos of life.

Mercy and Forgiveness

If you, O Lord, should mark iniquities, Lord, who could stand? But there is forgiveness with you, so that you may be revered. Psalm 130:3-4

The beauty of my son's newborn baby was the initial point of association. Chubby, rose-flushed cheeks, she was a portrait of innocence. Put a little pair of wings on her and a sweeter looking cherub could not have been found. Holding her in his arms, my son remembered a Renaissance painting he had recently seen, in which cherubs were rather hauntingly hovering over a coffin." While there are some ancient links of cherubs with death, I offered the suggestion that what he had seen might have been a representation of the Ark of the Covenant, with cherubim covering the mercy seat as described in Exodus 25. Here, in the holiest place of the tabernacle, God orders Moses to set the Ark with the dictate that "You shall put into the ark the covenant that I shall give to you." We learn later that the ark will house the ten commandments and other laws that God intends this special tribe to follow. As God says in Deuteronomy 6:2 "…these statutes and ordinances… you and your children and your children's children" are called to observe, so that you will "fear the Lord your God all the days of your life… so your days will be long." In other words, the way to live begins by loving God (v.5) and walking in right relationship with others.

However, it is my observation that God looks a lot like Jesus in this Exodus passage. Just above the commandments enclosed in the Ark, God insists upon placing a *mercy* seat. The cherubim will "overshadow the mercy seat with their wings" (Ex. 25:20). Could it be that God has the foresight of mind and forgiveness of heart to position mercy above the commandments: commandments God knows the people will often fail to follow? Could it be that the meaning of the Ark of the Covenant was captured with deep insight by the old song: "I'm overshadowed by his mighty love?"

Upon hearing my interpretation, my son said, "That is beautiful!"

> *May all my sins be overshadowed by mercy and forgiveness. May I grant that freedom to those who fail and offend me. Amen.*

Postscript
The Face of Forgiveness: Regrets to Nietzsche (2009)

Forgive us ...as we forgive. Matthew 6:24

She was the one person who knew the truth about my father's transgressions on the mission field some seventy years ago. This 95-year-old matriarch of service leaned as heavy on the table as the words she had to say. With lowered gaze and softened voice, she stumbled over Dad's offenses. Then her countenance suddenly brightened: "But your mother was a saint. Like Shadrach, Meshach, and Abednego she went through the fire and didn't smell like smoke."

My mother often read Lettie B. Cowman's book *Streams in the Desert*. Cowman sites Galatians 6:14 as a backdrop to the trials of the Apostle Paul and Silas in her October 17 entry. She writes in her typical disconsolate fashion, "They had asked to be meek and He had broken their hearts; they had asked to be dead to the world, and He slew all their living hopes; they had asked to be made like Him, and He placed them in the furnace." My mother wrote: "October 17 – the very best in the book – 1942." That was the year Dad told the truth. The Mission Board rightfully sent them home. Mom was no stranger to the fiery furnace. Then, in her late twenties, she must have shared this reading with her now elderly friend. I wonder if they wept together.

She bought this devotional for my father on their first Christmas in 1935. It was not meant to be a prenuptial promissory note. I find sad irony in knowing it was this very book that helped her endure the sexual improprieties of the man she loved. For Mom, a goodly part of her Christian sojourn was about suffering, trusting God, and the attempt to walk in the freedom of forgiveness. The smoldering ashes of dashed hopes from other offenses would leave the seven siblings smelling like smoke, but Mom would not let the pungent odor of unforgiveness linger. In that commitment, she was a saint.

My father was also a saint. Two years ago, I visited the Tanzanian village where my parents served. To my great fortune I interviewed seven elders in their 80's and 90's who came to Christ through Dad and Mom's ministry. They knew my father's heart. The common question I asked was: "What was my father like?" Without exception each person poured out accolades of praise and affection. They remembered him as one of the most loving missionaries they had known. Three of the seven emphatically told me, "Be like your father." In some ways, minus Dad's shadow-side, that's just what I hope to be.

Dad practiced what he preached about Jesus' last words: "Forgive them." My father was very compassionate. Time and time again the poor were seemingly ungrateful recipients of Dad's benevolence. During later years, when he invested in real-estate, the rich connived against him without remorse. Dad had the audacity to believe that love and forgiveness spoke louder than lawsuits and retribution. In times of family crisis he would make pastoral visits to those who had hurt him. He helped them without mentioning past offenses. Years later some came back to say thank you, others to seek forgiveness, and a few to find freedom in the love of Jesus Christ. "Forgive them." Those are powerful last words!

The philosopher Friedrich Nietzsche considered Christian virtue a manipulative means of "will to power." He distained apparent weaknesses like kindness and forgiveness. My family struggled with many sins and strained relationships that had the potential to devastate any kindred spirit among us. Anger, fear, frustration, hate, hesitancy to trust, demands for justice, and desire for vengeance all played a part in our relationships. Nietzsche, in his twisted way, would have loved that part of us.

Yet, there was a greater love that drew the members of my family together, and defined us. A *cross* stood at the core of our corporate heart. Notwithstanding the tears of separation, the years of counseling, the heartache of words and deeds that diminished us, and the face-to-face confrontations that empowered us, our faith in the hope of the cross became our salvation. As long as we could see the cross we would not be blinded by our brokenness.

Each of us fought for himself and herself; but we all knew we must also fight for the other in some ultimate story of forgiveness. We were raised on a host of biblical passages and parables that reminded us of our own need for mercy, grace, and forgiveness, so we could not simply point fingers. Somehow, we had to be ambassadors of reconciliation (II Corinthians 5:20) for each other. We had to learn how to "speak the truth in love…and grow up into Christ" (Ephesians 4:15). It is tough to turn toward the offender, state your case, and call for a new way of relating. We did our best to turn our swords into plowshares (Isaiah 2:4).

Forgiveness, we discovered, is not conditioned by forgetfulness, but it does require the determination to lay down our weapons of just retribution. Then our hands are free to open the door for restored relationship. But there are no guarantees. It takes two to tango, and trust must be earned. We are still learning the art of being "as wise as serpents, but as innocent as doves" (Luke 10:16).

The younger sibling, Jacob, plays some dastardly tricks on Esau. He spends years running, in fear that Esau will take his life. Now, the moment of accounting is upon him. Esau sees Jacob from a distance and runs to meet him. The younger shakes in fear, but the elder "falls on his neck and kisses him" (Genesis 33:4). Jacob in astonishment looks at his brother and says, "Truly, to see your face is like seeing the face of God" (Genesis 33:10). Like the cross, this is a scandalous picture of the power of weakness. Esau is a saint. There is no scent of smoke on his clothes!

The cross is an intolerable offense to most of us; not because a good man died, but because it seeks to expel the human desire for vengeance and appropriate retribution. We demand that everybody should get just what is deserved. That's only fair! But Jesus turns our sense of justice upside-down. The world stands by the Calvary cross to watch what Jesus does with vengeance and violence. As the old hymn notes "he could have called ten-thousand angels" and blistered his enemies with celestial wrath. But he didn't. The crowd is astounded by the absence of vengeance as Jesus cries out, "Father, forgive them." What strength is there in such weakness?

Retribution is much more gratifying than absolution. Yet Jesus invites us to "pick up the cross and follow" (Luke 9:23). He challenges us to be daring enough to believe that he has "overcome the world," which lives by sword of mouth and hand (John 16:33). Another world, another kingdom beckons us. In that kingdom, forgiveness trumps vengeance. In that world there is no greater gift than the power to birth new creation from the chaos of our lives. That world is at hand each moment the heart is hurt. I want that world! Its gaze is focused on the face of Jesus.

Someday the final snapshot of the Leaman clan will be taken. When all the stories are told and it is hung in the hall of history, our family framed will look like forgiveness. There may still be a lingering scent of smoke in the room, but salvation will be in our eyes. Send my regrets to Nietzsche.

Choices Come with Shadows

Again Jesus spoke to them, saying, 'I am the light of the world. Whoever follows me will never walk in darkness but will have the light of life. John 8:12

When the *mysterium tremendum* offers the light of life, we tremble, tremble, tremble! The cover of darkness is a comforting shelter. We can swim in those depths without fear of the unfamiliar ray of truth that could shatter our underworld. The deep can be a cold but convenient climate for resisting change. The warming beam of conviction cannot penetrate that space. We cling to the hope that our existence down beneath is beyond the Spirit that moves upon the surface of the waters. Our greatest fear is that the deceit of our freedom might someday be challenged.

And eventually, that someday comes. The sea erupts and we are thrust upward. There is nothing we can do about it. Suddenly, we are swimming too close to the light streaming from above. Our blinded eyes turn to the side and for the first time we behold that which the darkness could not expose. The shadow is cast. We gaze upon another side of self that the depths of an ego-centered existence had hidden from our hearts. Our freedom is challenged. In this light our lives must change, and we tremble, tremble, tremble. To face the shadow rather than chase the darkness is the choice we must make. We can never be the same. If we choose to dive deep to once again, and swim beneath the light, the weight of denial will become the curse of our being. Something of self dies in those depths.

The choice to let that light expose our true self will be disquieting. Either choice is going to hurt. Yet only one choice will make us whole.

Only one is the light of life. In that light we will tremble, and tremble, and then tremble yet again. The process of transformation can be painful; but have faith, for this is the path to peace. Plain and simple, it is risky business to swim the way of Jesus.

> *Dear God, may the mystery of your light dispel the fear of facing the monsters in my closet; the shadows of my other side. May transformation become an ongoing process of plainly and simply following the footsteps of Jesus. Amen.*

Compassion, Justice, and Borg

> For [God] delivers the needy when they call, the poor and those who have no helper. [God] has pity on the weak and the needy, and saves the lives of the needy. From oppression and violence [God] redeems their life; and precious is their blood in [God's] sight. Psalm 72:12-14

I am again reminded of Marcus Borg's distinction between being compassionate and working for justice. Borg contends that many Christians give to others under the banner of compassion, but relatively few take up the cross of seeking justice. It is easier to give than to get involved. Yes, the poor will always be with us if we merely give money to assist them in their plight, but the active voice against the injustices of a system that perpetuates poverty presents a more hopeful solution. The principalities and powers need to be challenged and changed if the poverty statistics are going to decline. It is so much easier to preach and teach about Jesus' priority for the poor than it is to actually take the time to understand the political dimensions of their poverty. My periodic letters to congresspersons are miniscule offerings of support in comparison to the task before us. Of late, I feel like the Spirit is calling me to fuller participation in healing this societal ill, but I balk because my time is consumed with my teaching career. It takes so much effort just to understand the issues. For now, I attempt to placate the disquiet by offering monetary support. At some point, however, I know I must do more.

It was your Spirit that motivated Gandhi to call the untouchables "Children of God." Likewise, O God, lead me to that cause of justice for the poor that pushes me beyond mere monetary transactions and thrusts me into the mainstream of activism that truly transforms. Amen

Contentment In Plenty and Want

I have learned to be content with whatever I have. I know what it is to have little, and I know what it is to have plenty. In any and all circumstances I have learned the secret of being well-fed and of going hungry, of having plenty and of being in need. I can do all things through [Christ] who strengthens me. Philippians 4:11-13

For whatever unknown reason, our cat Simon loves the texture of my briefcase. Even as I write she curls on it, relaxing in perfect contentment at my side. Paul writes in Romans 8 that "all of creation moans and groans for the day of redemption." Yet up to this point in Simon's life I have never heard a groaning sound. This feline already basks in the beauty of God's kingdom come to earth. Even more endearing than Simon's satisfaction is her gladdened response to my occasional caress on the nap of her neck. The reflexive, abbreviated purr that emanates from within is one of the most sweetly endearing sounds I know. Therefore, my fingers frequently slip from the keyboard to stroke her soft fur. The contact is simply the *purrrrrrfect* touch for both of us. An affirming and strengthening touch.

The assurance of the Spirit of Christ, God with us, is that existential stroke to the soul which emboldens us with an "I can do or get through this" approach to all the seasons of life we encounter. It is that faith which brings contentment and completes us with confidence. It brings proper perspective to the highs and lows, the times of plenty and times of need. In all the "lots" or "littles" of life the Christian can find solace in the faith that fills us with a "we are not alone" conviction. This certitude can carry us beyond the limits of what appears to be reasonable. I cannot write as one who feels the peace of this *purrrrfect* touch in every circumstance. I can only say that in those moments when belief silences doubt, I do experience contentment in the "Christ who strengthens me." I sit by Spirit's side upon the case that carries all the briefs of my life. I long for the reassuring stroke of "God with us." She is the soft touch in hard times that frees me to live in the fullness of every moment.

> *Great Spirit who speaks through all of your creation, keep me ever grateful for every picture of tenderness life provides. Help me to paint a picture of your grace for someone today. Amen.*

Create A Clean Heart

Create in me a clean heart, O God, and renew a right spirit within me. Psalm 51:11

Whose responsibility is it to create this clean heart? How does the renewed spirit happen? Christians would claim that the cleansing comes from outside of ourselves, and that the third person of the Trinity empowers the spirit's re-creation. The conditions of transformation are the sincerity of our prayers and a genuine desire to change; but God works the transformation. God tidies-up the mess we made because we want God to do what we can't.

Sometimes I am more Buddhist than I would like to admit. The Buddha said, "Be a lamp unto yourself." He was not concerned with questions regarding the reality of God. He declared that if one practices mindfulness in light of the Four Noble Truths and the Eight-Fold Path, one can *willfully* change his present and future reality.

In the matter of addictions, my experience as a counselor and pastor has shown me that no matter the countless prayers and confessional tears an addict sheds before the feet of Jesus, healing will not occur until the addict determines to follow a long and lengthy series of disciplined steps towards renewal. The transformation is more about personal volition than prayerful petition. Of course, one can always point to those occasional radical conversions that immediately and miraculously turn someone's life around. We can argue that it was God's response to prayer that brought the addict his new heart. But the norm points to the final, desperate, and determined choice of the addict's desire for freedom. He must be willing to hold the lamp and start walking toward the light, "one step at a time." The addict is the only one who can let the light shine upon his darkness.

Yet, does the addict's ability finally to see and follow the light have its source within because there is a greater source outside?

> *O purifier of desire, grant all who struggle to walk in your way, the harmony of heart and mind that finds strength and solace in the hearing of 'work out your own salvation in fear and trembling, for God is at work within you, both to will and to do His good pleasure" (Philippians 2:12-13). Show me the scale that rightly weighs the measure of my effort and your grace. Amen*

Postscript
Vanquished in 2005

How, O God, did I come to this state of constant turmoil? Not a day passes without me anguishing over some aspect of my relationship with you. I once loved you, but now I hold you at bay and doubt not only your love for me, but for all of humanity. There are times when I wish that you did not exist, that I would not have to factor you into the realities of life. My morals and ethical decisions would still be characterized by love and compassion for others. I could get along without you; yet I live in this endless conflictual relationship with you. I am like the proverbial husband who says he can't live with his wife, yet neither can he live without her. Sometimes, I just wish you would walk out the door. But the fear of you doing so is more terrifying than anything I can imagine! Even while I am desperate for you, I distain the thought of you. This impassioned pursuit of knowing you wearies me to the point that I wish we had never met. I am so tired! It takes so much energy to hold you at a distance; yet to draw near to you would deny the reality of my questioning heart. The mystery of your supposed goodness makes little sense to me. Some would say that my greatest sin is my attempt to understand you, for to do so reflects a fallen desire to be god. But your greatest sin is to tease me with grandiose creative powers and facades of unconditional love without granting me the capacity to understand enough to endear you to me. I am so afraid to die in this state of disbelief, for in doing so this love of yours which eludes me may leave me for eternity. God, if I am to be driven senseless in my devotion to you, please make some sense to me.

I am exhausted by my sojourn. Ten years ago, I said that I would leave the ministry if I could not discover an understanding of you that would allow me preach with integrity. Five years ago I left the ministry. The battle for my soul still rages within. I am vanquished. I do not want to raise another arm of protest against you. You may have won the fight, but you have not won my love. You have only frightened and defeated me. How many times over the years did I attempt different types of spiritual disciplines as an attempt to feel your presence? Every prayer tactic I knew about, I tried. You alone know, as I felt myself slipping from your grip of grace, how many times I prayed, "create in me a clean heart, O God"; "don't take your Spirit from me"; "Lord, be merciful to me a sinner." Who failed whom?

One thing I do know is that I feel like a failure, and I fear the consequences of my faltering ways. I desperately wanted to get my act together so that I could inspire a desire in my boys to love you and live for you. But now I fear that my own doubts and questioning spirit may have negatively influenced their openness to you. I want to be convinced enough to convince others, for I know that a critical heart and cynical mind does not change lives for the better. I have seen many lives transformed when people understand your love for them. Yet here I am, still confined by my caviling. Doubt wallows in self-centered, myopic meanderings. Life is supposed to center around you and others, not around me. The problem is that I don't even like you right now; but I am afraid to live now and forever without you. Life has to be about both of us.

Depart from Evil; Pursue Good

Depart from evil, and do good; seek peace, and pursue it.
Psalm 34:14

Clear out, exit, get off – a few synonyms for "depart" plucked from the pages of the dictionary. In other words, don't lounge, linger, or dillydally around the nefarious. Don't doodle with, deny, or attempt to defend any iniquitous thought or action contrary to the wholeness that God desires for human relationships. Hold Mother Teresa's confession close to heart: "The reason I picked-up 40,000 dying people off the streets of Calcutta was because I knew there was a little Hitler inside of me." Seemingly insignificant choices that lack integrity become tiny channels of seepage, which in time flood with forces of self-interest, leaving destruction in their wake. Exaggerated? Yes, but little movements create potentials impossible to predict.

Chase, follow, hound, pursue the good and that which brings peace. Tail, trace, track the footsteps of those who exemplify the heart of God. Lean towards the good; "set your mind on things above" because they are meant for the best of life below. "Whatever Is true, whatever is noble, whatever is right, whatever is pure, whatever is lovely, whatever is admirable—if anything is excellent or praiseworthy—think about such things…and the God of peace will be with you" (Philippians 4:8-9). You are an image of God – a co-creator of goodness. Your thoughts create your destiny and build a well of peace to which many will come and draw, because the virtuous life is not simply running from something, but running toward Someone.

Dear Jesus, in thought, word, and deed keep me running towards you. Amen

Devoted to the One I Despise

No one can serve two masters; for a slave will either hate the one and love the other, or be devoted to the one and despise the other. You cannot serve God and wealth.
Matthew 6:24

I am not sure that I buy all the hype about receiving greater rewards in heaven because you have given more on earth. As one who refuses to believe in hell, and hopes that heaven is a reality of love that cycles through our temporal existence on earth, I am not too invested in that which is to come. Maybe that's why I have invested in others, here and now. Throughout my life I have followed the Biblical guidelines for financial giving: usually between 12-15% of gross annual earnings. There are still times when I get a check and immediately think, "Cool, I don't really need this. Who can I give this money to?"

However, I find it strange that in my later years I am struggling with a more self-serving attitude. Retirement is just a breath away and the economic picture is looking bleak. I must confess that I've been getting angry at God. *God* is the One who set-up the system of good and evil, celebration and sadness. It seems that every month a catastrophic event strikes somewhere in the world. The Almighty seems to expect me every time to respond with open pockets. "How much more can I give, God? You designed it. You fix it. Put a 'steady as you go' on those tectonic plates. Get your own people out of life's inevitable messes. Don't be laying this 'can't serve two masters' guilt trip on me! You want more of my money to repair your damages. Take care of your own lilies in the field, birds of the air, and all Creation's children.

As crazy as it sounds, sometimes it seems that I am devoted to the One I despise.

> *God, I pray that I will ripen with age. Do not let me shut off the life-giving flow of your Spirit and let self-protectiveness have her spoils. Don't let me become bitter and brittle. Let me be that tree that remains flexible and bears even better fruit through every stage of growth. As my years lengthen let the branches of my benevolence broaden. Amen.*

Postscript
Scaring Myself: A Crazy Kind of Communion (2005)

Man is a hungry being. But he is hungry for God. Behind all the hunger of our life is God. All desire is finally a desire for Him.
　　　　　　　　Alexander Schmemann (*For The Life Of The World*)

"God help them," I said aloud. A television news program had captured images of those abandoned to starvation and cold after the earthquake in the Himalayan Mountains. The thought came quickly on the heels of that prayer: "I don't even know how to pray to a God who is supposed to be sovereign, yet allows this kind of tragedy. Why does God ask me to pray for the victims of the very system God created? O, I do pray, but I don't get it. I don't like it.

Sometimes my cynicism frightens me.

I challenge: "Why is savagery and suffering such a high priority for you? Survival in this world depends upon the death of another life form. If you knew that's the way it would be, with your incredible imagination and the infinite number of options at your disposal, couldn't dying at least have been less painful?"

I taunt: "No, it appears you thrive on suffering. Then, when your creatures don't comprehend the purpose of this embattled adventure called life, and they cannot conjure the adoration you seek, you banish them eternally from your presence."

I conclude: "Of course, our fears will not let us rest with such a dastardly deity, so we deduce that pain, suffering, and the whole job-lot of evil is our fault. Surely God, as the Genesis garden story suggests, you must have had a better plan in mind."

I curse: "Yet, you are the First Cause who foreknew the realities of human choice, so it is to you that I raise an indignant fist! Creation must be the consequence of a narcissistic being who thrives upon the creatures' worship and praise."

I cry: "You made us for yourself! You made me for you. In you I am supposed to 'live, and move, and have my being.' I am, so the scriptures say, to 'delight in you, so that you will give me the desires of my heart.' Well, sometimes 'I have no song to sing' and that scares me. You scare me!"

My lips are tight and my arms fall limp. There is longing, but my palms do not turn upward with expectation. It is hard to swallow the body and the blood. I am ravished by hunger, but there is no sustenance in the sacrament. I feel so conflicted. Condemned in the midst of this crazy communion.

Dominion and the Divine Image

Then God said, 'Let us make humankind in our image, according to our likeness; and let them have dominion over the fish of the sea, and over the birds of the air, and over the cattle, and over all the wild animals of the earth, and over every creeping thing that creeps upon the earth. Genesis 1:26

The ancients would erect images of their gods in the village or city to remind them of the deity's influence. The idol indicated the realm of rule. Our Hebrew storyteller wants his reader to consider humankind's realm of rule to be the global village that has been fashioned for him-her. (The word "Adam" originally meant male *and* female). Humanity was created to reflect the will and way of the Creator. But just how does that Designer express dominion? To answer that question we must peer into the mysterious nature of the Deity. One theological perspective imagines the God of Noah, the God of Abraham, Isaac, and Jacob, as one who, on a whim of wrath, wipes out those who fail to follow his almighty will. It's a "kill the infidel approach." And humanity has without hesitation consistently imitated that image. On the other hand, the Hebrew scriptures do paint pictures of a loving and faithful God, who led the people "with cords of compassion" (Hosea 11). Through the prophets, the Deity demands care for the stranger, provision for the widow, and advocacy for the oppressed. Yet, for the prophets, the stranger, the widow, and the oppressed were those within their own tribal society.

The Deity's kingdom did not transgress the borders of the privileged (who confined God within their own theocracy and salvation history), was not significantly expanded until Jesus' radical reforms. Then the image of God was truly reflected, and the ancient hope that Israel become an instrument of blessing for the whole world was finally fulfilled.

Now, the symbol of the cross reflects the will and way of God that we are called to follow. *Now dominion looks weak – like being a servant.* A strange definition of rulership, indeed. Yet, if we all chose to live that way, could there be anything more powerful for good? All of creation would sigh a smile of relief! Heaven on earth would be the here and now.

> *O God, sometimes you seem to have the two faces of Janus; even more the multiple faces of Vishnu, Shiva, and Brahma. Human interpretations of your likeness have given you carte blanc to do whatever, to whomever, whenever you want. We have couched your freedom under our finite inability to comprehend your "thoughts that are not our thoughts and ways that are not our ways." We have named you the Unmanifest Manifest in light of sacred texts that depict you as the arbitrator of great evil that we must somehow place within the framework of your work of preserving good. Yet, so much of what you do does not endear yourself to us. So finally, God, we pray that you are like Jesus. His life reflects an image of ourselves that we would like to mirror. Amen.*

Don't Bungle This One

The quiet words of the wise are more to be heeded than the shouting of a ruler among fools. Wisdom is better than weapons of war, but one bungler destroys much good.
Ecclesiastes 9:17-18

Dad comes to mind with this reading. He often said, "A word to the wise is sufficient." Sometimes he used it as a weapon of warning. It was his transliteration of the Biblical injunction to "take heed." And if I didn't take heed, my father would tell me to choose my own "weapon of war" – tearful free will within a closed paternal system! – which would then be painfully applied to my bottom. Teddy Roosevelt said, "Speak softly and carry a big stick." Well, I soon learned that those little paint sticks can hurt as much as the big sticks.

I remember Dad offering me a different word of wisdom when I wanted to make a quick, unnecessary purchase: "When you see something you really want, wait two weeks and see if it might be something you can live without." I abandoned many unwise, impulsive purchases thanks to Dad's cautions. I am a richer man, literally and spiritually, because I did not throw this bit of wisdom to the wind.

Perhaps the discipline of waiting is a good practice when it comes to words as well as ways. Wait two weeks to see if that person really needs to hear your words.

Thumbs up to a dad who steered me from being a "bungler [who] destroys much good."

> *I am grateful, O God, for a father who taught me the wisdom in delayed gratification; whether that be in relation to the purchase of a product or the desire to speak in a untimely fashion. May that spirit guide all statesmen and women of the world who truly do wield the weapons of this world. Amen.*

Postscripts In Praise of My Father
Promises to Remember (2006)

I saw you tonight, Dad. I was sitting in the second pew to your left, snuggled under mother's right arm. You were joyfully leading the congregation in "Standing on the Promises." The people could never sit for this one. We stood. You sang with abandon. Heading toward the final chorus, your countenance glowed with the excitement of a child on Christmas morning. Nobody did it like you, Dad! Grinning with glory, your hands waved us toward the closing crescendo with palms upturned, as you signaled for everyone to hold that final note as long as each could "stand on the promise" of sustained breath. Yet, one by one, singers would drop out, gradually fading into breathless silence, while a lilting, lyric voice floated high above all others. The beauty of that lone, strong tenor note persisted. We smiled. That's what good Mennonite singing does, you know: it makes you smile. Thanks for the memories, Dad, and thanks for standing on those promises!

Over "This?" (1999)

"Here," the man said, as he handed me a *Stamp's Quartet* gospel tape. Out of courtesy for his enthusiasm, I reached out.

"I'm over this!" my soul whispered. "Musically and theologically." He seemed oblivious to the awkwardness of the exchange, and appeared unable to resist.

"Take another one. If you like J.D. Sumner, you'll really get into this!" Patronizingly, I kindly refused the offer.

"Thanks, Bob, but I really don't listen to gospel music much." We said our good-byes, and I drove off chastising myself for borrowing a tape, which, if lucky, might make one go-round in my tape deck. After all, "I'm over this."

Then I listened to it. Many of the songs were distantly familiar, and the words flowed from my mouth more freely than songs I'd been singing in recent years. My mind floated down forgotten streams of memory. Annual trips to the Harrisburg Forum for an evening of gospel singing were one of the few ways Dad and I spent time together. We shared a certain harmony in song. When the Happy Goodman Family or the Blackwood Brothers took center stage, and the pianist's fingers shot across the keyboard with the ease of a flying bird, something took hold of us – and I'm telling you now, our souls sang. Dad had a lyric voice that could shame a sparrow to silence, so when the first tenor topped-out on a high "C", guess who couldn't help but match him? Dad and I. Then J.D. Sumner would sink a bass note, seemingly far below the keyboard. While dad knew better than to attempt that extreme, I was quite sure that my slur of low guttural sounds came close.

The auditorium, its seats curving around to the sides of the stage, appeared immense to a little guy like me. I got a kick simply from running up the stairs to the top deck and circling all the rows. The singers got smaller as I got higher. What a thrill it was to imagine myself front and center, with hundreds of people admiring me!

All too soon, the songs would stop, the clapping would cease, and the curtains would close. Yet all was well. There was solace in knowing that just a few minutes down the road, I would fall asleep with dad beside me. The next moment of consciousness would bring the crunch of stones under tires as we pulled into our driveway. What a comforting sound. Could I even count the times I feigned sleep as my father carried me from the car and tucked me under the sheets?

That J.D Sumner tape has been played far beyond one go-round of my tape deck. Listening to that gospel quartet takes me home. And, frankly, I don't ever want to "get over this!"

Dumb Reasoning

Now may the God of peace, who brought the great Shepherd of the sheep, our Lord Jesus, back from the dead through the blood of the new everlasting covenant, perfect you in every good work as you work God's will.
Hebrews 13:20-21

Did both Hebrew and Christian writers of the Bible intend to characterize God's people as sheep? They were certainly aware of how dumb and helpless sheep are. A sheep fears running water, cannot upright itself if it gets belly-up, cannot defend itself before a predator, does not properly groom itself, is susceptible to parasitic invasions, and blindly follows a designated leader. The metaphor of people being the sheep of God's pasture does not paint a pretty picture of humanity.

On the other hand, those biblical scenes where the sheep follow their shepherd is a stroke of literary genius for conveying God's role in the divine-human relationship. The Shepherd of Love leads with his staff to pull his sheep from the briars that would entangle them, and he wields his rod to beat off the wild beasts. The Shepherd knows how to lead his flock to green pasture and still waters. He knows the safest paths for their sojourns, even those that precariously wind around the highest cliffs, and then dip to the lowest valleys where danger lurks unseen. He combs their matted braids, and rubs oil on their heads, face, and ears to deter parasite infections. His call is their comfort. They hear and heed his voice. They follow. Yet theirs is not a blind faith. They know instinctively the peace their Shepherd brings. Only the dumbest of the dumb would not follow the good Shepherd's lead.

> *Dear Jesus, in thought, word, and deed keep me running towards you. Amen O God, although this request taunts reason; help me to be as dumb as I need to be. Amen.*

Postscript
Please Sarah, Don't Laugh (2010)[1]

I search for her amidst scores of books. She is not hard to find. She carries her treasure between water-stained covers, but at 173 years old, her spine is broken, and every brush loosens orange flakes of leathery skin. Her name, *Martyrs Mirror*, is barely legible. A rubber band encircles her girth. She reminds me of the ninety-year-old biblical character Sarah, sitting in withered wonderment between barrenness and fertility. O, she has been with child countless times, but can this worn woman yet again fulfill the fancy of her creators? Can this matriarch of martyrdom give birth to another youthful Origen who ran into the streets to give the ultimate sacrifice? Can she still conjure the spirit of Truken Boens, "daughter of Wilhelm Boens of Antwerp," who went a second time under the waters of baptism only to be burned at the stake (411)?

I reach for her. To hold her is to cherish the hopes and memories of parents whose greatest honor would have been to be recorded in her pages. In our Mennonite family, m*artyrdom* was God's highest calling; second best was the mission field. My parents chose the latter and glorified the former. *Martyrs Mirror* was home for us. She was formed by

---

[1] As published in *Tongue Screws and Testimonies: Poems, Stories, and Essays Inspired by The Martyrs Mirror*. Ed. Kristen Eve Beachy. Scottsdale: Herald Press, 2010, 262-264.

the dusted blood of martyrdom, with a mission to seed the passion of future generations who would willingly "subject their young members to His yoke" (xiii).

I reverently leaf through the pages. Her lap is a storyland of faith. One narrative in particular stirs my soul. The subtitle reads: "Jacob Dirks, and his two sons, Andrew Jacobs and Jan Jacobs, A.D., 1568" (645). I have two sons. One carries the middle name of Andrew. My boys are in their thirties, but they never age beyond "my beloved." Mr. Jacobs and his boys "fell into the paws of the wolves at Antwerp." They were charged guilty simply for being Mennonite, and all three went to meet death by fire. They were tied to the stake. Andrew's bride-to-be watched and wept. Just before the piles were ignited, Mr. Jacobs asked his children, "How do you feel my dear sons?" His tenderness grabs me. My eyes moisten. Those words . . . those boys could be mine. I can see their faces. What a terrible-sweet moment of affection and pride. The executioner strangled each of them, and their drooping bodies were burned, "thus sealing the truth with their blood" (646). Though frightened by the thought of martyrdom, my fragile faith is momentarily emboldened. I am born again. I tell this old tome that I will be strong, as they were. I will forsake all for Jesus. She bursts forth with victorious song. Unlike Sarah, this ancient vessel knows that age need not close the womb.

But does *Martyrs Mirror* exalt me too soon? So many proved to be faithful to the end with no regard for what that end might be; could I do the same? Would I hold heaven's joy so dear? Would I really be a Germanius of 170 A.D., who stood flint-faced before the wild beasts (75)? I'm frightened by the midnight cry of a bobcat! Might I be shamed by the likes of Hans Simeraver who was "imprisoned for the divine truth," and ultimately shared the fate of John the Baptist (383)? Perhaps, if I had the option, I would plead for the quick and painless blade of the guillotine – just do it! It is dangerous to prolong the decision of this doubter. Sarah might laugh again. I find no great gain or glory in torture. I see no need for me to say, with Jan Wouters upon his whipping, "O flesh, methought you must now suffer" (816).

Dare I whisper in the executioner's ear, "You can damn me for heresy, but don't drag me, dunk me, or slowly strangle me?"

It's foolish for me to think I would have any say.

Oh, I too easily vacillate! I peek through death's door with a chilling reluctance. Is death merely an exit, or is it an exodus into new life? The Apostle Paul writes of a sublime eternity that "no eye has seen, nor ear has heard, nor human heart has conceived" (I Cor. 2:9). I like this, but I don't *know* this. Do I fully believe, like Abraham, in a promised land that far exceeds the wonder of warm lips, clasped hands, and the familiar love I have known this side of the Jordan?

John wrote *Revelation* during Domitian's rampage of persecution in 96 C.E. He was attempting to encourage his people. He envisioned a peaceful paradise where God himself will wipe dry the tears of believers (Rev. 21:3).

"Yes, yes," I say, "I long for the solace of heaven's kindness." But the moment is quickly shattered. I read on in *Revelation* and discover that those who are "cowardly and faithless" will be cast into "the lake that burns with fire and sulfur" (Rev. 21:8). The cruelty of such vengeance repulses me. Should fear of the God I am supposed to love inspire me to martyrdom? I want to recant for the sake of all sinners. I want to be Moses who challenges God when the Almighty refuses to forgive the idol worshipers. God wants to kill them, but Moses has the tenacity to declare that if God does that, then "blot me out of the book that you have written" (Exodus 32:32). The protests of the patriarchs are meant to save many lives. Will my audacious pleas rescue anyone from perishing?

Would all this questioning sustain me in the face of prolonged suffering? An open book, a blank page, and Sarah watches intently. What will the records show: "I recant?" Or, like Martin Luther, "Here I stand, I can do no other?"

Please, Sarah, don't laugh.

Duty and Reward

The one who plants and the one who waters have a common purpose, and each will receive wages according to the labor of each. For we are God's servants, working together; you are God's field, God's building. 1 Corinthians 3:8-9

Perhaps it is time in my life to begin thinking about "wages." Until now, I have lived and loved without thought of reward; a simple do good for goodness sake, a kind of dharmic, dutiful approach, was all I needed. Perhaps my apathy in regard to reward is rooted in an underlying doubt that heaven even exists. Since I know precious little about a place called heaven, but resonate with the prayer to bring the kingdom of love and justice to earth, it has always been relatively easy for me to relegate thoughts of reward to the back seat. Duty-filled living did the driving.

This has served me rather well throughout my life, but as I get older I find myself wondering if faithful living receives its rightful reward – not just now, but then. And I feel a taint of resentment burn my veins when I think there might not be some ultimate compensation for pious rather than self-indulgent living. It is not that I stand at the front of the line after a twelve-hour workday, grumbling about the boss' generosity when he gives the other workers – who spent only an hour tugging at grapes in the vineyard – the same exact pay he gave me for laboring all day. No, Jesus' parable promises that God graciously grants to each what is needed rather than deserved. I recognize that under the cover of "duty," I must have hidden an expectation of reward that I never resolved. Now I must face the irony of wanting some eternal cache, while doubting the reality of the eternal itself. Perhaps in this period of my life, where the temptation to waver feels more compelling than in the past, I need to believe in some ultimate wage-calculation, some commendation of effort that comes from outside myself, to keep myself faithful. Duty alone doesn't do it anymore.

> *It seems so much more pious to do right without pining for reward. Yet, O God, there is part of me in these latter years which desires the distinction of differences in your sight. Look mercifully upon that member of being which cannot be comforted by simply living for the best welfare of the other; that part of me that seeks to draw my own categories of distinctions destined for curse or commendation. I pray that I will not be found poking for splinters in my neighbors' eyes when my own are blocked by even bigger pieces. Help me to believe in the mystery of your benevolence beyond what "neither eye hath seen, ear has heard, or the heart of man conceived." Settle my soul, O God, so that every action is balanced by hope and proper intent. Amen.*

Ecological Justice

Therefore the land mourns, and all who live in it languish; together with the wild animals and the birds of the air, even the fish of the sea are perishing. Hosea 4:3

What is the "background of Hosea's *therefore?* Verse four of this passage goes on to say, "There is no faithfulness, no love; no acknowledgement of God in the land." Idolatry and murder shacked-up in the land of Israel. God told the prophet Hosea to marry a harlot as a compelling metaphor of how Israel had prostituted her original passion for God and pursued other lovers. While there is no historical evidence of numbers of birds and mammals perishing at this time, the author does offer a powerful picture of the interconnectedness of God's creation. The human heart and hand do impact the other treasures of God's kingdom. When we bow to something less than the Creator, our selfish behavior plays havoc with the environment, making it no longer a haven of rest. The Great Spirit inhabits all of creation.

Has this not been the story of our obsession with materialism? We have not paid genuine allegiance to the God we say we trust on our dollar bills, but have put our trust in everything the almighty dollar can buy. Our idolatry has polluted global ecosystems. Feminist theologian Sally McFague contends that we have failed to understand the interdependency of our *oikos* (household). In her essay "God's Household: Christianity, Economics, and Planetary Living," she states:

Neo-classical economics has one value: the monetary fulfillment of individuals provided they compete successfully for the resources. But what of other values? Two key ones, if we have the economics of the entire planet in mind, are the just distribution of the earth's resources and the ability of our planet to sustain our use of its resources.

Our consumerism does not make room for disciplined lifestyles, or even for serious dialogue that could speak to the concerns McFague raises. Our demands have stripped the planet of resources simply to satisfy our insatiable appetite for bigger, faster, and more. Now even the birds of the air and the fish of the sea suffer loss and live at great risk. To forget God is to forget life. How many more nights can we shack-up with the harlot before the *dis-ease* of our spiritual epidemic destroys us? To what extent have *I* been stricken?

O God, I ask that you do not allow me to be too much at ease with my lifestyle. Give me the courage to put myself in the places of dis-ease; places like your church, where I am continually challenged to question the values that drive me. There I am frequently reminded to purposefully resist being conformed to the society around me. In the fellowship of believers I am encouraged to seek transformation of my mind, so that I might live and love like Jesus. Do not let me be comfortable. Keep me in that creative state of tension between the good I am called to do and the actual good I do. Amen.

Postscripts In Praise of Creation

Brethos (2006)

The sun lurks behind looming clouds.
A dismal overcast cools the morning air.
My shoes dampen in the wet grass
As I hold my arms close to my chest
With regrets that I chose the short sleeves.
But the warmth of wonder fills my world
As I walk around the perimeter of our yard.
I see the first fruits of a small mulberry tree that I have been nursing for two years.
Finally, she will share her bounty.
It appears that the blackbirds have also noticed the gifts she bears,
But they will be my only competition.
No one else thinks mulberries are worth stained fingers and purple smiles.
I remember that as a kid I would place an old sheet under the tree, climb her limbs, and shake them until the blanket of white was covered with this poor man's fruit.
I felt pretty rich myself.
The grapevine has proudly unveiled her clusters.
There are more than ever this season.
Ah, look here. That blueberry bush I planted last year is also showing signs of plenty.

And those wild wine-berries and raspberries came back so well from their pruning.
They will be ready for picking in another month.
My bowl of cereal will soon be more colorful and pleasing to the palate.
There is hope and expectation even on this dismal day.
The clouds cannot hold back the sun indefinitely.
I breathe deeply.

Our House (1997)

Now tell me little wren as you fly hither and thither
Do you know I hung that house for a home of one like thee?
As you flit in flight and frantic chirps fill the silent air
Are you conscious of the curious one sitting over there?
Over where...?
Over where the skin bumps up from the gentle breeze
Where lawn meets woods with vista through swaying trees
Where I have hung my hat and for hours have sat
Watching little ones like thee.
Should I tell you little wren,
That I hung your house for me?

Elemental Spirits

If with Christ you died to the elemental spirits of the universe, why do you live as if you still belonged to the world?
Colossians 2:20

Simple answer, Paul: because it is so much easier. If my biological drive is to live, one of my elemental desires will be to procure and protect that which I believe will help me survive. My Creator conjured this mix of matter and spirit, which seems necessary for the perpetuation of human life. The "elemental spirits" to which Paul refers in this passage, however, reflect early Gnosticism's refusal to accept Jesus as incarnate. For them, God could not be dirtied by the soil of bodily human experience; so heavenly hosts emanated from God, becoming progressively more like us, thereby bridging the gap between the holy and the profane. For the Gnostic, the goal – which only a select few could understand – was to attain the secret wisdom of the *mysterium*, completely disassociated with the stained, evil reality of matter.

For Paul, it was not secret knowledge for a select few that saved, relationship with a God who dared to get down and dirty with us in the person and body of Jesus Christ. Affirmation of the incarnation, scandalous as it was to Gnostic factions, opened the door to a transformational relationship with God in Christ. Any "elemental spirit" that separated us from the image of God in Christ, and confounded the meaning of Jesus' act on the cross, Paul considered a heresy that put human wisdom, pride, and self-survival above the simple faith, humility, and servanthood so basic to being Christian.

Christ, grant me the gift of death, so that I might live anew. Amen.

Embracing the Shadow

By the tender mercy of our God, the dawn from on high will break upon us, to give light to those who sit in darkness and in the shadow of death, to guide our feet into the way of peace. Luke 1:78-79

Death looms over us in the midst of life. In our ever-present awareness of the transient nature of existence, we are plagued with a haunting sense of vulnerability. The vibrancy of reality will someday succumb to the still darkness of the unknown. And we shudder before that shadow. Religion is humanity's best medicine against the fear of annihilation. It holds forth a picture of hope in its claim that the cold, closed eyes of mortality will yet open to the warmth of God's immortal presence. Therefore we need not fear the shadow. In fact, from a Christian perspective the shadow can be faith's cheerful reminder of the resurrection hope that spurs a Pauline-like confidence of "for me to live is Christ and to die is gain." Jesus is the "tender mercy of our God" who brings the light of God's love to the shadowlands of our existence. Inasmuch as we will to live, love, and forgive like Jesus, our feet will follow the way of peace on both sides of the grave.

God, give me the courage to embrace the shadow. Amen.

Postscript: Resurrection (2008)
Who Can Rouse the Deadly Silence:
Garden Stories Of Resurrection and Hope

Genesis 1-3

The earth was...

- without form

-amorphous

-shapeless

- without structure

- and void

-empty

-useless

- without purpose

- darkness was upon the face of the deep

-foreboding

-black

-deathly silent

Would this be all that would be?
What spirit watched over deep darkness?
Who can rouse the deadly silence?

And God said, "Let there be."
And there was...
-light and land
-sky and sea

-feathered and finned

-mammals and man

-goodness and growth

Out of nothing sprung a garden where

-love's light dispersed deep darkness

-shouts of life shattered the silence

-mortal mirrored the Immortal

God took chaos and sculpted new creation.
Then the tree, the choice, the sin
Humanity was lost in broken relatedness.
Yet we are found in another garden of grace
Just beyond the gates of our estrangement.

Mark 14:32-42
And "God Saves" kneels in the garden.
The whole world waits on tip-toes.
The disciples fail to watch. They
fall silent
quietly doze
-   yield to restless slumber
die to the moans of the Master.
The hour is darkened with memories of
- love scorned by unmitigated hate
- repentance stunned by revenge
-new life muted by threats of death.
This night is without form.

-The depths of loneliness
-Unspoken betrayal
-It fits no mold.
This night is void.
-The epitome of emptiness.
-Shattered dreams.
-It makes no sense.

Would this be all there would be?
What spirit watched over this deep darkness?
Who can rouse the deadly silence?

And Jesus said: "Not my will…"
He was dragged from the garden rock to Calvary's hill.

There he met
curses and cries
laughter and levity
spears and spittle
vengeance and violence
crosses and quakes
death
the silence screamed
Hope died, but the consensus was mixed.
Some with believing hearts wept "GOD-IS-NOW-HERE."
Others with unbelieving taunts sneered "GOD-IS-NO-WHERE."

There is yet another garden of grace
Just beyond the scandal of the cross.

John 20:11-18
And Mary stood weeping by the garden tomb.
Someone had stolen
the love that had formed her
the meaning of her existence
the light of her world
The darkened cave was void of life.
no corpse to perfume
no body to touch
no witness to the emptiness
It was midnight in the middle of her day.

Would this be all there would be?
What spirit watched over this deep darkness?
Who can rouse this deadly silence?

Jesus said, "Mary" and
-silenced the swirling chaos
-stifled the haunting doubts
-sweetened a new dawn

The sound of his voice roused this world to hope because
-hate is hushed by love
-fear falls to faith

-death can't hold the final word

-The light shines and the darkness cannot overcome it

-I am the resurrection and the life.

-*Believe me.*

Envy and "The Other"

If we live by the Spirit, let us also be guided by the Spirit. Let us not become conceited, competing against one another, envying one another. Galatians 5:25-26

That which separates us is the almost instinctual need to see someone as the "other." Competition seems a necessity of survival. There is a natural desire to scrutinize the moves and motives of others in an attempt to gain a concrete advantage, or at least an air of superiority. Such is the spirit within us. The smallness of that spirit is largely responsible for the way we put others down to lift ourselves up. We do not naturally have the desire, the sensitivity, or the capability to strike a balance between a healthy, interdependent ego, and the illusion of an autonomous self. Enslaved to a false freedom, we lust for power and whatever will satiate the desires of a self out of line with love.

The solution to our dilemma lies outside ourselves. It rests in relationship with the Divine. And so we pray with David, "Create in me a new heart, O God. Renew a right spirit within me" (Psalm 51). In this prayer the chains of bondage are broken, and we see clearly our interdependence with others and our dependence upon God. This is true freedom, and its expressions can be observed in love, kindness, and the empowerment of those whom we previously viewed as the other.

Dear God, May I not be so eager to compete as to complete the aspirations of your new creation in friend or foe. Amen

Footwashing: Body and Soul

> [Jesus] came to Simon Peter, who said to him, 'Lord, are you going to wash my feet?' Jesus answered, 'You do not know now what I am doing, but later you will understand.' Peter said to him, 'You will never wash my feet.' Jesus answered, 'Unless I wash you, you have no share with me.
> John 13:6-8

The shocking message of the master-servant is: "Peter, if you do not get this part right, you are not on the right path. Your stumbling and scarred feet will soon start to sting with the infections that redden the flesh of those who lust for the power of privilege, and despise the empowering service of love. Now, stick em' out here, Peter!"

Deeply regretting the "never" he wished he'd never said, the impulsive disciple who wanted nothing more than to please his master, shoved both feet in front of Jesus, and pleaded, "Well, if that's what you mean, then wash my hands and my head and …"

"That's alright, Peter. If you bathed today the rest of your body is clean; just the feet, Peter, just the feet."

We were separated: the men and the women. Twice a year in the Mennonite church my father pastored, this passage from John was read, followed by a brief devotion, and then we all filed to designated rooms at opposite sides of the sanctuary. As a child, I questioned this gendered division, which, mingled with a certain mysterious solemnity, created a stir of sexual anxiety, as though there would have been something terribly wrong if men and women went to those rooms together. At puberty, I understood. Until then, I had never noticed Lydia's long, shapely legs that so graciously carried her well-contoured figure. There was something certainly something wrong with me, that I would stoop so low as to imagine Lydia lifting her skirt high enough to unsnap flesh-toned nylons. "My God; my gaze!"

It was difficult to appreciate the sacredness of this ritual. I often had the chore of filling the large plastic basins with water. Then, so the worshippers would not immediately withdraw their feet from the chilly waters, I would carefully place a small heater into the container: scarcely a job that felt sacred. Many farmers and factory workers attended our church, and they did not attend to their feet in any form or fashion! One could not help but notice bent bones, twisted toes, and bits of stocking stuck to gnarled, yellowed nails. A missing toe was particularly fascinating. We washed and dried one another in silence. Closed lips was probably the best wisdom in this sacred situation: no doubt we were all thinking how gross each other's toes were!

And then, years later, I got it. The grossness was, in a way, the point. We come to one another with feet plastered with all the muds we have mucked through, along with muddy, dirty thoughts, and everything that has tempted us from following the footsteps of Jesus – and we thrust our feet forward to receive the cleansing we know we need.

Yet, there is more. Washing the feet of friend and foe (I have seen quarreling married partners moved to mutual acceptance through this ritual) is not merely a matter of spiritual renewal, but physical touch. It is through flesh on flesh that the spirit is set free. Jesus rejects the dualism of physicality and spirituality; both are God's good gifts! Healing happens in the union of the two. It happens through the one who tenderly lifts feet laden with the mire of broken relationships, and washes them with waters of hope. It happens when that person dares to look upon the unsightly, and dignify it with the gentle caress of water and towel. It happens when a man exposes his feet to another man who holds and handles them with a mother's care. What an incredible act of vulnerability! It feels so unnatural, this ritual, about as far away from macho as a man can get. Here, the scary becomes sacred; so frightening that we Mennonite men could only handle it twice a year.

In the days Jesus trekked through Galilee, the lowliest of all the household servants had the job of washing the guests' dusty, dirty feet. There are over 7,000 nerve endings in our feet. Imagine all the sensations sent through brain and body. No wonder the warmth and relaxation of a foot massage feels so heavenly. Jesus knew the predicament of our feet. So, with humbled heart and helping hand, with the water and towel, Jesus taught us that to soothe the feet was to soothe the soul. That's podiatry at its finest. If you don't mind, I think I'll warm another basin of water.

I pray that my feet will follow in your path, dear Jesus; that they may bear the dust and carry the stench of service. And may I never be so proud as to resist the chance to humbly lift my feet before my brother or fail to reach for his when the cleansing waters are rightly warmed for accountability. Amen.

Forbidden Flesh: Can't Touch This!

If your hand or your foot causes you to stumble, cut it off and throw it away; it is better for you to enter life maimed or lame than to have two hands or two feet and to be thrown into the eternal fire. Matthew 18:8

The whole heavens would stand aghast! And the gates of hell would rattle with excitement as this guilty child of God confesses to fingers that fondled forbidden flesh. Much better for me had I severed "it," or my hands at the wrists, than now to serve Satan's fodder for the flames. Why did the tree of life-giving pleasure have to stand in the center of a man's garden? God made sin so easy: how diabolical!

My father applauded a Mennonite man who accepted castration as the final antidote for impurity. That was far too literal and loony for me. As infrequently as I could permit myself to engage in masturbation, the guilt and fear were relentless. Rumors of unrepentant sinners were legion. Had it already handicapped my spiritual stature? I remember writing "never again" on the underside of my mattress during my early teenage years, only to have my mother discover the convicting phrase when I was a young adult.

"Someone must have done something he should not have done," she said. Thank God by that time it didn't matter to me if she identified me as the guilty culprit of our five brothers.

Postscript

The Folly Of Never

I shoved the relish dish across the table.

"I hate olives. I'll never eat another one!" With a wink of the eye and a smile that shone as brightly as his balding head, Grandpa Eshelman put out a challenge.

"Melvin, if you eat seven in a row you will like them forever." My loud protest belied an inner desire to please him, but my "never" triumphed on that day. One day, however, I choked down the seventh olive, and the prophet's words were validated. Does "never" ever linger beyond the morning's mist?

My nevers, puffed-up with self-righteous stubbornness, have often suffered deflation. For example, it was a matter of fact that smokers were destined for the Pit, so I pledged never to touch the weed. Once, when our neighbor lit his cigar, with five-year-old indignation I scolded, "Mr. Harvey, if you keep smoking those things you will go straight to hell." Now I periodically puff a cigar. I guess neither of us will need matches down there.

"Those Beatles look like girls with their long hair and floppy bangs. I'll never let my hair get like that," I declared. That was the early '60's. Then came the 70's. My hair was shoulder length. And when it came to pleasuring myself, why did I ever say, "I'll never masturbate again." That resolution inevitably climaxed in guilt and demoralization.

Other nevers have come and gone with the decades. Some years back I pointed out that the use of leaf-blowers was the epitome of laziness and expediency. I mean, who can't take the time to put a little muscle behind a rake? This Christmas my boys bought me a leaf blower.

Yesterday, as leaves scurried from a windstorm, I thought about the olives. These days, they are so much easier to swallow than thoughtless words.

> *You have created us, so the Scriptures say, "male and female" and all the varieties of gender expression on the spectrum of sexuality. You affirmed our sexuality, God. Our gender distinctions are good. Help us to know how to celebrate these gifts in healthy and holistic ways. Amen.*

Postscript
Praise of Sexuality

Beauty
February 12, 2006, For Joan's 51st birthday

Beauty.
The beholder stands awestruck
Raptured by this reflection of the Creator's goodness.
Stunned by seeming flawlessness
The mundane stands from afar with wanton gaze.
To draw near without invitation offends nature.
Such perfection holds a hint of the forbidden.
One need hesitate in these holy moments
Like the pause before the first step in a fresh field of snow
The sanctuary of silence before a setting sun

The smallness felt beside the towering mountain.
Beauty is blemished by the conspicuous
So, I set my gaze in secret.
As one standing at a distance
Fantasizing lack of permission
I wait; I watch; I wonder
Breathlessly captivated by the views.
Heaven is in your lips.
My earth quakes in your contours.
Your eyes are my future.
You are -
Beauty.
Still amazed,
Mel

Postscript

Joy of Man's Desiring (2010)

My twenty-mile trip south to Christiana, Delaware, is serving a dual purpose: to visit a friend in the hospital recovering from brain surgery, and to find a highly recommended book on forgiveness. Our pastor visited the hospital a few hours ago, and I don't want to needlessly weary the patient. So the book search is first on the agenda.

A quick stop at the Barnes and Noble reference desk goes nowhere. I pass up the offer to order the book. A few steps left of the counter, four cushioned chairs are neatly positioned around a small table cluttered with assorted books. Ah, a place of respite for sixty-year-old hips still smarting from all those sudden twists and turns in the church, and adult-versus-youth flag-football games. I was the only grey-haired senior to bear the flags and fling my body in the path of oncoming, side-stepping adolescents. It felt great – yesterday.

Today, I plop into the pillowed chair with an indiscreet sigh of relief. God bless Barnes and Noble hospitality. A woman in her mid-seventies is sitting across from me. I don't mean to be nosey . . . but I am. What is the name of the book she is reading? I see the big, red heart that symbolizes love on the outside cover. Maybe it's a "how to love your great-grandchildren" book? Then noticing the cook book section directly behind her, I concluded it must be a collection of recipes for a healthy heart. Nope, wrong on both accounts. A closer, but not too obvious gaze, gradually brings the title into focus: *I Love Female Orgasms*.

I lean back. Phew! My imagination kicks in. I picture an elderly woman lying on her bed in a fit of frustration wishing her partner's little blue pills had done the trick. On the other hand, maybe her partner's tricks were no treat at all.

"Ok Leaman," I whisper to that lively little man in my head painting the bizarre, "let's put that image to bed. Her reality will soon be yours; and then, as now, there will be prettier pictures of desire."

Andre Botticelli singing "Jesu, Joy of Man's Desire" filters through the sound system; and suddenly it's just there – an instantaneous sadness, an unwelcomed sense of loss. Some 34 years ago my friend Chip sang that song at our wedding. We remained friends throughout the years, but recently he lost a battle with alcohol. He lay undiscovered for several days in a Colorado apartment. Remembering Chip's deep, baritone voice stirs melancholy in my soul. I stay for a while; but to linger in the doldrums would be to insult the celebration of enduring love.

Was there ever a more beautiful bride? My Jesus, she has been the love of my life and joy of my desire, after desire, after desire. Her soft face, full lips, and contoured frame can still slay me flush with rousing embarrassment. Please, good God, grant my wife another 20 years of loving orgasms! May desire pulse in our veins 'til death us do part! I was born for love.

An infant smacking his wanton lips rouses me from my reveries. Tiny hands flail and fumble with longing as the mother settles into the chair beside me, breast and babe discretely sheltered beneath a white, quilted blanket. Desire can be so pure. With a coo of contentment, the infant finally sleeps.

Solace envelops me. My body breathes. My shoulders sink. I slip ever deeper into the soft-cushioned chair. I am lost. Yet, I am found in the remembrance of a true brother – Chip Fahs – a beautiful bride, and a new-born babe. The joy of desiring engulfs me. I am at peace.

From First Kiss to Faltering Faith

I brought you into a plentiful land to eat its fruits and its good things. But when you entered you defiled my land, and made my heritage an abomination. Jeremiah 2:7

This passage is part of the Holy One's lament, distraught over Israel's pursuit of the god Baal. God is puzzled by the people's progressive loss of their youthful passion for true holiness. The Almighty is angered by the fact that the priests are not asking, "Where is The Lord?" Jeremiah must deliver the message that the consequences of their choices will be devastating.

This story, to some extent, is mine. I, too, have lost the exhilaration of the first kiss, and the innocence of trusting God. The black-and-white snapshots that so strikingly delineated the thoughts and actions of the Divine now appear blurred to me. I cannot, except through the lens of Jesus, say that the more I see of God the more I love God. Not that I bow to idols; but ambiguities have stifled the words of praise which once fell freely from my lips. Some would say that I should sing again because ambiguities simply express the wonderful mysteries of God. But my lips remain shut. My faith does not venture that far. There are times when, like Adam and Eve, the desire to know feels like it will mean my death.

O God, I sometimes pine for the first kiss. The relational dimensions of making love, truly knowing the other can be so difficult. Amen.

Postscript
The Mystery (2001)

Shallow
It can be shallow to see self as the center.
Is my kindness to draw others to me or to someone with much deeper channels?

Narrow
It can be narrow to make self the mark of the way.
Is my perspective to give others mine or the eyes of someone who sees a much broader vision?

Finite
It can be arrogant to rest comfortably in the confines of finite wisdom.
Is my comprehension to be trusted or is there One of more infinite discernment?

Creative
It can be indulgent to genuflect to the creative side of human expression.
Is what I create and conjure complete or is there a Creator who completes me?
To which shall I bow...
The shallow, the narrow, the finite, and the creative, or
The deeper, the broader, the infinite, and the Creator?

Shall my trust be in self or The Self?

Why do I stand on the sands peering contemplatively upon the sea?

Why do I sit on mountaintops gazing breathlessly across the skyline?

It is not that which man or woman has made that captivates my spirit.

It is not that which I call mine or you can claim as yours.

It is before the mystery that I fall awestruck.

Basking in the beyond, I stand beside me.

To which shall I bow?

Is life about me, or the mystery

Handle with Care

Be wise when you engage with those outside the faith community; make the most of every moment and every encounter. When you speak the word, speak it gracefully (as if seasoned with salt), so you will know how to respond to everyone rightly." Colossians 4:5-6

I loved those little red sweats pants. Not just for the way they swaddled my two-year-old in warmth, but even more for the slogan that ran down the side: *Handle with Care*. That slogan always reminded me that the people I encounter, both physically and in theological dialogue, whether agreeable or disagreeable, should always be handled with care. Rather than seeing that person as "the other," he is a brother who, just like me, longs for love and needs right relationship more than being right. Admittedly, in the midst of disagreement, the slogan might be forgotten; but mindfulness of this truth will set us both parties free to be "quick to listen and slow to speak." Only then can the truth of head and heart be heard.

    I had the opportunity on two occasions to work for a week with the Lakota Indians in South Dakota's Pine Ridge Reservation. There I learned a new phrase: *mitakuye oyasia*. It means we are all brothers and sisters. The famous Lakota Indian Chief, Black Elk, offered a wonderful image of the circle of love and the Indian world of the spirit in his statement, "The birds build their nests in circles because they have the same religion as us." There really is no one outside the community of love. To this I will cling with "every moment and every encounter."

> *Dear Jesus, in all of the ways that you would, let me handle all your children with care. Amen.*

Postscript
From Generation to Generation: Do You Know, My Son?
For Tadd (son) and River (9 month old grandson), Christmas 2011

Do You Know...
That in as much as you love him now, I have loved you since then
The way you savor his subtle smile, is my joy again and again
All your thoughtful ponderings to protect his innocent heart
Have been mine for you, my son, from the very start.

Do you know...
That as much as you treasure the firsts, so long does my love last
Your anticipation of yet to comes, are my present and my past
The delight that you experience in each cuddle, coo, or crawl
Have been mine for you, my son, from your first to my final draw.

Here Comes That Dreamer!

They said to one another, "Here comes that dreamer."
Genesis 37:19

They did not mean this as a compliment. Rather, it was their condemnation of a character who, whether in innocence or insolence, shared his dreams with his older siblings. That might have been simply amusing, except for the fact that in these nighttime flicks Joseph's brothers held the short end of the stick, while little Joseph had the upper hand. No one likes to have the deck shuffled only to find his card on the bottom, particularly when one is an experienced and better player. Reversal of realities feels threatening. It's the way the senior college athlete feels when an incoming freshman is about to steal his position – particularly if the new kid has a cocky attitude.

Dreams like Joseph's coming true happens to be a consistent theme in Scripture. The elder, experienced, empowered, and expected leader will bow to the younger, the novice, the weak, and the least expected. This surprising turn of events will spur those with entrenched power to protect their status and privileges by eliminating the threatening other. Such "others" are the likes of Moses, Joseph, Jeremiah, and Jesus.

Switch genders, and you'll have a list of unlikely barren women who, after much failure and distress, offered their dreams as desperate petitions to the Divine. These less than adequate women, like Sarah, Rebekah, and Hannah, gave birth to nations through children of great esteem. God loves to surprise those who dare cling to a dream that clearly goes against the grain of normality.

Tomorrow, we celebrate Dr. Martin Luther King, Jr.'s birthday. As was true of Joseph's brothers, white folk with prestige and privilege did not appreciate this visionary's message. His voice was not welcomed.

Protecting the powers that be, they killed the prophet; but the dream could not be denied. It was held in the heart of One who could conquer evil with good. The dream lives on, and the dreamer comes again, and again, and again.

> *I bow in gratitude, O God for all who have been exemplars of justice; those whose dreams drove them to risk the scorn of the powers that be and the scourge of peers who refused to see the vision. Thank you for their daring determination to set the kingdoms of this world upside-down; those who counted the cost and just kept on going. Give me a dream much grander than myself, so that I might realize my dependence on you and interdependence with your children. Amen*

Hubris, Humility, and the Heart

O Lord, open my lips, and my mouth will declare your praise. For you have no delight in sacrifice; if I were to give a burnt offering, you would not be pleased. The sacrifice acceptable to God is a broken spirit; a broken and contrite heart, O God, you will not despise. Psalm 51:15-17

The haughty heart has no place for God. It insists that the Infinite should demur to finitude's comprehension of the cosmos, its meager attempts to fathom the mysteries and solve the ambiguities. Clenched fists overwhelm hands raised in praise, as words of whispered gratitude give way to teeth grinding out despair. Thanksgiving for what has been is consumed by the flaming desire of what *should* be. The demand to eat from the tree of knowledge becomes the root of evil and the ruin of relationship. A fear-based, hardened obsession for exacting Truth quashes the relational fluidity of Trust. And before long, the finite being feels justified in his despair, and reckons the Infinite quite deserves his anger. Ever so slowly hubris swells within his heart. Disenchantment with God becomes righteous indignation on behalf of humanity held at arm's length from the mind of the Deity. Blinded by rage, he becomes more righteous than God. He sees clearly; God should shop for glasses.

The indignant rebel fails to see that his anger is motivated by self-centered preservation. He wants to *know*, so that in the knowing he might feel safe, saved, and accepted into the kingdom of God. Hubris hides behind a false mask of self-righteous indignation, and with this, sin crouches just outside the door. At some point, prideful anger will provoke irresponsible deeds, and then the man might realize that he has shut out the very Spirit of God that could have restrained him. Now, perhaps he comes home with a broken and contrite heart. If so, Infinite Love cannot help but open the door. Thanks be to God.

> "Have Thine own way, Lord; have Thine own way. Thou art the potter, I am the clay. Mold me and make me after Thy will. While I am waiting, yielded and still." Adelaide A. Pollard

It's Second Nature to Me Now

His divine power has given us everything we need for a godly life through our knowledge of him who called us by his own glory and goodness. Through these he has given us his very great and precious promises, so that through them you may participate in the divine nature, having escaped the corruption in the world caused by evil desires. 2 Peter 1:3-4 (NIV)

She has "grown accustomed to your face," so much so that "it almost makes the day begin." Eliza Doolittle, precocious Cockney flower-girl in the Broadway hit, "My Fair Lady," continues in song: "It's second nature to me now; like breathing out and breathing in." There is within each of us an impulse as natural as breathing out and breathing in: the impulse to do whatever we need to do but often shouldn't do; the impulse to appease a drive for self-preservation, or pleasure. The spirit of self-preservation is an essential and God-given aspect of being human. However, when that spirit desires self-preservation or pleasure at the expense of another, it conflicts with our Creator's intention for relationships. Christianity claims that at this point we become powerless in our attempts to squelch desire's demands. Our lungs have breathed its poison, and blood has thickened in our veins and fogged our minds, until we willingly allow denial to steer us from true thought and action. What seems second nature to us now, saps the energy we need in order to seek and know what is right. In our relationships with others, we can easily sink to an almost subhuman level.

Over a period of years, poison ivy vines twist their way up to the treetops and block the nourishing sunlight. The poison must be pulled out at the root, or at the very least cut at the base of the tree. On the day the vine is cut, the poison ivy leaves still look green and healthy. Death looks alive. For a brief season corruption can appear convincingly lifelike; but eventually its fruit will die on the vine. In times like these, divine power can expose and diminish the seductive nature of that which binds us. The Scriptures dare to suggest that "you [we] participate in the divine nature" through the acknowledgement and acceptance of Jesus' commission in our lives. The empowering presence of God's spirit assures us that we are not alone in our struggle to balance the God-given instinct of self-survival with the spirit that gives life to and through others. When we look at Jesus and yield ourselves to his life-giving spirit, we share access to a mysterious energy that far exceeds our personal capacity to strive for goodness and serve the right. Christian hope lies not in what we can conjure, but in the conviction that there is a God who loves us, lights our way, and energizes our spirit to move toward goodness when we have exhausted all reservoirs of hope. That's the nature I want to breathe.

> *O, Divine Breathe, fall gently upon my being and fill me with your living words, so that I might walk in your way when I have no will to follow. When the reservoir to do right is dry and my desire to run for the mirages of my own making consume me: call to my remembrance the "precious promises." Do not let me forget the mystery of your divine nature which completes and empowers. Let your spirit have full sway. Amen.*

Jesus Vetoes Violence

The Spirit of the Lord is upon me, because [the Lord] has anointed me to bring good news to the poor. [The Lord] has sent me to proclaim release to the captives and recovery of sight to the blind, to let the oppressed go free. Luke 4:18

Jesus' fellow Jews considered themselves to be oppressed captives. Their long-awaited Messiah had never come, and the children of God continued to languish under Rome's authority. The Jews labored under a pseudo-freedom: they resided in their homeland, but they had no control. Therefore the holy city was not at peace. The people were at Herod's mercy. At his nod, his soldiers could sweep the Jerusalem streets clean of protesting riff-raff, or suffocate the Jews with repressive restrictions. Zealots dreamed of the day when violence would crush the Romans and make way for the promised peace of Zion.

Even today, peace achieved through power is the American way. In his book, *The Upside-Down Kingdom*, Donald Kraybill writes: "The seductive power of nationalism seeks to wrap God's blessing around national destinies that have nothing to do with Christian faith. Some Christians will prostitute the Gospel by justifying military crusades under the flag of God's blessings." How often have we, in stride with Israel's ancient war hymns, marched off to war singing "God Bless America?"

Perhaps the most-loved portion of this Lukan quote from Isaiah 61 was that the Messiah would usher in "the day of vengeance of our Lord." On the Sabbath in the synagogue, a rabbi would read portions of the Torah, Wisdom literature, and the Prophets. Jesus was selected to read this passage from the Prophet Isaiah. Was it a coincidence that he neglected to read the phrase about the Lord's vengeance? Or was he stating from the start that the battle would not be won with fighting fists, but with outstretched arms and open palms? Jesus was possessed with a strange spirit. He vetoed vengeance. He wept over Jerusalem's inability to let go of the myth of violence. Surely, Jesus said, "those who live by the sword will die by the sword." They killed him!

> *Free me from my desire for vengeance, O God. Let me be strange enough to stand for the truths that put you on the cross. Amen.*

An Exit or an Exodus

A Quest For God Amidst Doubt

So I say to you, ask, and it will be given you; search, and you will find; knock, and the door will be opened for you. For everyone who asks receives, and everyone who searches finds, and for everyone who knocks, the door will be opened.
Luke 11:9

She sat by the sliding door in the kitchen. Sunlight streaked her silver, gray hair. "Mom," I queried, "do you ever doubt God?" Perhaps it was a silly question to ask a woman who had witnessed both miracles and misery, but could still sing "Great Is Thy Faithfulness" with unwavering belief. Why couldn't I sing with equal conviction?

A brief silence ensued. She lived a full life and raised seven children; she had a lot of history to review.

"Don almost died in Tanganyika, and David in the States. Sometimes it was hard to understand God's purposes as I watched my children struggle with various issues in their lives. The church had its challenges too!"

My mother's passions were family and her church. Dad pastored a Mennonite congregation in York, Pennsylvania for many years. They gave their all to God, whether on the mission field in Africa, or in the local ministry.

"I've cried out to God countless times for wisdom and understanding. But, Melvin, I can't say that I ever doubted God."

Shamed by her strong assurance, I wondered how I could ever confess the depth of my doubts. She wouldn't understand. It was safer to skirt the surface of my uncertainties. Mom's kind of faith felt like a distant memory to me. It's embarrassing to admit that my faith had faltered, even though the difficult times I encountered seemed trivial in comparison to the things my mother had endured. Frederick Buechner suggests that "doubts can be the ants in pants of faith." Well then, mine were fire ants. Too many tough questions inadequately answered. I felt overwhelmed and guilty.

I was the pastor of a growing United Methodist Church where people were excited about their sojourns of faith. Lives were changing, and love ran deep. Small groups were being formed, while talk about relocating and building a new facility was in the air. They were energized, but I was exhausted. The fresh breath of God no longer "fill[ed] me with life anew." I felt breathless. The right words were there, but I lived and moved between the waxing and the waning of faith. How long could I stay there and serve with integrity? It was December of 1994, about a year and a half after that talk with mom, that I penned this prayer:

> *While faith is waning for me, O God, can I yet have faith in you? Will you hold me or let me go? Do you consider doubt the termination of relationship or transformation? Does my struggle for faith negate the effectiveness of my prayers; your faithful response? Will you yet pray for me when my prayers to you are confounded - perhaps infrequent? Can I trust your love for me, or do you thrust me aside in my doubt and diminish my ministry?*
>
> *Would you dare to accept the possibility that I may not be losing my faith, but rather expanding it? If you would, perhaps I could!*
>
> *God, I have no other passion beyond that of following you, but when you are breaking out of my package, I must be*

free to explore and find you somewhere beyond the familiar trappings that once tied everything together. I fear that you will not be faithful; that I will somehow step beyond the boundaries of your acceptance; that transformation might tear us apart rather than tender our love. I do not want to lose you, O God, but I cannot find you fully in the confines of the faith to which I cling. Is to search, to stray? Can I really trust that to seek is to find? And if I stray too far in the seeking, could you yet find me?

Some of the tenants of my faith are fraying at the edges and the garments of salvation are a bit tattered. Does Christocentricism imply exclusivism? Have I duly and deeply considered the character and conclusions of other religions? Why would a God of love ultimately judge so harshly those who never asked to be born? How can life be affirmed as a gift from God when so many experience life as suffering and conclude that our years are merely the testing grounds that determine matters of eternity? Is the claim that "Christ died, Christ was raised, and Christ will come again" a creed I can trust? Just how much are you involved in the daily affairs of my life? Does the reality of my questioning suggest that I have been duped by relativism?

Oh God, please hear my commitment to you, yet also acknowledge the call that compels me to answer these and many other questions. If by January 1996 I cannot find a more comfortable integration of my faith and my questions, then I will consider leaving the ministry.

The years passed, but the doubts didn't. It seemed that the harder I prayed, the heavier my heart became. Frequent confessions and constant petitions for renewed joy brought little peace. I shared my struggles with a few special friends, but this did not thwart the eventual disconnect between my calling and my questioning.

I attended seminars on world religions, including a graduate course in Judaism taught by a rabbi, in an effort to be open to the Spirit from all sides of the theological fence I also participated in the Billy Graham School of Evangelism. My experience there proved to be a turning point. I was greatly impressed by a particular speaker's enthusiasm, dedication, and theological surety, and upon returning home, I preached a similarly fiery sermon. That experience only exacerbated my discomfort with attempts to wrap truth in a package of certainty. Personal integrity demanded that I preach from a more open, questioning spirit.

Church attendance increased. We bought property to relocate. The "promised land" was just over the horizon; but I wasn't sure if I could cross over Jordan with my people. I was a leader with too many questions. Growing churches need pastors with answers, don't they?

I experienced times of deep, inner turmoil during the next two years. If I left now, the congregation would have to adjust to the relocation *and* a new pastor. After fifteen years of ministry, wouldn't a sudden exodus feel like betrayal? But I could no longer preach with heartfelt conviction, and it seemed dishonest to linger. I didn't know what I was going to do, but I knew that I could no longer embrace the vocation I had pursued for more than twenty years. The following poem captures some of my inner conflict. It was written in August 1999, two months after I took a voluntary leave of absence from the pastorate.

The thoughts of eternal consequences envelop me.
The soul has no solace in ceaseless questioning.
It is the canvas that waits impatiently for the artist's flair.
It is the promise of joy that invariably lies just around the corner.
I live with the fear that I may, fall to the pit, if there be one.
I live with the even greater fear of leading others into the fire.
There is no room in the sanctum of the saints for mistaken perspectives.
There is no place in the City of God for misinterpreted promises.
But either I cannot or will not quell the questioning and disbelief.
But if I do not or will not, the end is frustration and discontent.
The search, practiced with whatever integrity I command, goes ever on.
My God, is this an exit or an exodus?
Am I merely leaving or am I going to some place?
Is this a dead end or is there a promised land just around the corner?

An exit or an exodus: how do I see it now? Perhaps it has been a bit of both. I felt I had failed God and family in my exit from the ministry. How could a third-generation pastor let doubt defeat faith?

The prayer I had written in December, 1994, expressed the fear "that transformation might tear us apart rather than tender our love." I vacillate between the distance my decision has created and a longing to be held again. It's a real mix. Yet, there are times when God has come intimately close amidst the chaos and despite the distance. It is my hope that the Holy One determines to make this exit an exodus. God doesn't delight in dead ends, does he? Grace has to be greater than that! I am praying that this exit leads to entrances. Hopefully, grace is leading me home. What that home will look like remains to be seen.

Winds of transformation sweep across the pages of my life. What may come as I turn the next page? It seems that even my current employment as a professor of religion is somehow providential. The story of my landing this position sounds like a serendipitous saga of grace. Perhaps the "promised land" is not always an end as much as a process; we move simultaneously within as well as toward. "I don't know, Mom. What do you think?" The sojourn continues.

> God, even while I am drawn, I would like to feel the joy of knowing your work within me. It seems that heaven can be an endless hallway of closed doors. My knuckles are bloodied from the knocking. Peace is as impermanent as the distance between one door and the next. I look forward to the day when my trembling finds the peace of your "good pleasure."

Light of the World: A New Year Reflection
January 12, 2012

When Jesus spoke again to the people, he said, "I am the light of the world. Whoever follows me will never walk in darkness, but will have the light of life. John 8:12

Light reveals reality. It quells the anxieties of imaginations that quicken under the cover of darkness. Light is hope for the disheartened soul. There can never be a gloom so encompassing that a glow of light cannot pierce it. No matter how deep the darkness, the smallest flicker reassures. Seeing the light is always a forward-looking experience. With backs to the blackness, primitive humanity gathered around the fire and flashed their flaming sticks at nighttime predators.

Each New Year people around the world celebrate the hope that the darkness that enveloped their past will not define the reality of their future. The sparkling fireworks are splatters of promise against a blackened sky; serendipitous blasts of grace that refuse to let that which was, be all that will be. Whether the New Year is rung in with bellows of intoxicated laughter at Times Square, or prayers on bended knee at a village church, worshippers of all clime cherish a common hope that tomorrow will transcend yesterday; that veins warmed with inebriating spirits are indicators of better days ahead; that the deities who hold both night and day will grant goodness in the new year. God cannot help but be present within the "hopes and fears of all the years" that accompany worshippers on their annual pilgrimages to sacred shrines. May heaven's light, the good works of God's love for all creation, be embodied in us throughout 2012.

Light of lights, like the dawn of a new day upon the darkest night break through any blindness that cannot perceive hope. Grant us courage to set aside those withering wine skins of yesterday that feel so familiar to us. Those cups of faithfulness or failure have already been poured. The smack that lingers from the past has no claim over the taste of the opportune future. Enlarge our hearts, so as to be ready to hold the new wine of the coming year. Amen.

Little Man with a Melted Heart

Zacchaeus stood there and said to the Lord, 'Look, half of my possessions, Lord, I will give to the poor; and if I have defrauded anyone of anything, I will pay back four times as much. *Luke 19:8*

Does any story more pointedly capture the transforming power of love? His Jewish contemporaries despised the fact that they were puppets of Rome, yet Zacchaeus enlarged his own purse by collecting Roman taxes from his own people. Not only that – Zacchaeus knowingly exaggerated the tax and pocketed the extra cash. Who could be more hated and outcast in the Jewish community than he who sold himself to his oppressors? He was more untouchable than lepers. Zacchaeus chose his disease!

None of that mattered to Jesus. Powerfully curious about the touted prophet from Nazareth, Zacchaeus had come out from his cold and calculating isolation to risk mingling with the crowd. When their eyes met, Jesus did what one was never to do. Completely contrary to Middle Eastern etiquette, Jesus invited himself to dinner. Zacchaeus doubtless had few opportunities to play the host, so he said yes and held his breath. By the time the meal was over, love had melted his heart and new life had been breathed into his soul. As the Apostle Paul writes, this little man was "transformed by the renewing of the mind" in a big way. Jesus had come to seek not only the poor in pocket, but also those who lived in poverty of spirit.

Dear Jesus, help me to look for a Zacchaeus today and each of my tomorrows. Give me the sensitivity to know when the other longs for, but lacks the boldness to ask for a one-on-one heart-felt exchange. Then, let that meeting of hearts be life-giving to both of us. Amen.

Love Measures

If I give away all my possessions, and if I hand over my body so that I may boast, but do not have love, I gain nothing. 1 Corinthians 13:3

Love forms easily on the lips, but is hard to live. Giving away one's possessions in a grand gesture, or offering oneself to the martyr's fire, is one thing; but love practiced on a *daily basis* — that's something else. The mundane aspects of communication afford us countless opportunities to deepen our love. Our words are but wind-driven leaves if not rooted in love's fertile soil. It is as simple and hard as the old saying, "don't talk of love; show me." Those best able to measure my love are the ones who, inch by inch, mark my daily footsteps. Those who live under my roof or work by my side. *They* can tell you if my love is lip or life service.

I want to be remembered as a man who loved deeply, freely, and frequently. In that light, these thoughts came to mind on April 12, 2001.

There is but one thing I long to leave in this world: a legacy of love. If that is the story I leave behind, then my gift will not be lost in my going forth. Someone's tomorrow will shine brighter because I played some small part in his or her yesterday. Today, I am keenly aware of an overwhelming desire to wrap my arms around the world. Relatively few will feel the warmth of my words or deeds. My world is fairly small. But even so, I will not welcome death unless I live and leave a legacy of love.

> *May the words of my mouth, the meditations of my heart, the means of my lifestyle, and the manner in which I walk, be acceptable and pleasing onto you, O God. And may your judgment of me be bundled in mercy. Amen.*

Postscripts In Praise of Love and Family

The Family Framed
(Written in 2008 by Joan Linkin's husband, Mel)

Tucked into the hillside, camouflaged by daunting weeds and the creeping vines that hide cracked panes and crooked frames, sits an old, faded green cottage. In years gone by this tiny, wooden, two-roomed structure served as summer home for an elderly Florida couple. Northern breezes were welcomed relief from the scorching southern sun. Some fifty seasons have come and gone since their last trip to this paradise. Over the years a collection of farming tools rusted in cobwebbed corners. Broken toys and seemingly worthless antiques cluttered dusty floors. The mystique of this abandoned summer house lured curious children, for whom it was a Narnia-wardrobe of irresistible fascination, where they rummaged through dresser drawers, cabinets, and boxes filled with intriguing treasures. It became imagination's sanctuary, a place to create memories. Old tricycles, tattered bodies of dolls, and corroded instruments for cutting, sawing, and measuring – all became keepsakes. And all is now gone. The rooms are empty, the floors lie bare. Perhaps someday these walls will house a few goats, and they will keep the foliage from engulfing this miniature-sized homestead.

The children are now in their thirties, but the marks of their presence still line the edges of the door frame that separates the rooms. There, etched in pencil, scribbled in ink, or boldly noted in magic marker are the heights and names of the notables who could not resist the chance to write their way into infamy. These innocent recorders of family history were not so foolish as to forget the four-legged, beloved creatures that trekked up the hill with them. Abby, the pet goat, stood only an inch or so taller than her canine friend Sandy in 1977, but both fell about 8 inches shorter than my son Tadd's December, 1978 thirty-inch mark on the opposite frame. On the right, the lineage of friends and neighbors creep ever closer toward the ceiling: Nathan, Burn, Betsy, Matt, David, Ann, Robert, and Chris all join Mark for a 1977 measurement. The wall of history on the other side reads Joan 1959 standing two inches above her son, Toby in 1984. In 1964 Robin towered seven inches over her little sister Joan. Other markings include additional measures of Tadd and Toby in 1984 and 1987 respectively, with their father, Mel on one side in 1984 losing by six inches to their uncle Mark in 1977 on the opposite frame. Mel always did stand short.

These empty rooms can fill you. Come in. Be silent. Let your senses soak in the ambiance. You might hear anything from the sounds of hoofs and panting dogs to laughing children; you might smell powdered bottoms, bodies ripe from play, and mother's perfume on little girls who, of course, were always bigger than truth would tell. You might see sparkling eyes, warm embraces, and competitive stares. These vacant rooms are far from empty. They are full of the formative moments that have made us who we are. Come in. Pull-up that time-worn chair. Sit for a while.

Cold Lips: Warm Love
(February 9, 2010)

Anticipation of the beauty that dawn will bring keeps me stirring throughout the night. The morning light does not disappoint. Glory glistens just outside my window. I want to play in this blanket of white all day. Although the work of life has me snowed under, I cannot resist the chance to slip on my boots, throw a few seeds to the birds, and ask Joan to join me for a stroll. Surely, God must smile upon our excitement. The Psalmist declares, "Delight yourself in the Lord." How much louder can praise be than a silent breath of deep gratitude? Cannot a canopy of baby blue sky, blending with crisp, cool air and knee-deep snow, bring the soul into God's house as much as any Sunday morning scripture? This great God does speak softly in the written word, yet She does not shy from shouting in the windblown woods. Worship fills my heart as I walk hand-in-hand with the lady of my life for 33 years. We walk down winding roads, through fallow fields, under bending trees, and over frozen streams. We walk and we talk, but it is the silence that makes this morning's worship music. The rhythmic crunching of frozen snow under feet comes to a sudden halt. We turn toward the gaze of the other. Love is warm on cold lips. God smiles. I pray for another restless night.

New Hearts?

I will give them a heart to know that I am the Lord; and they shall be my people and I will be their God, for they shall return to me with their whole heart. Jeremiah 24:7

The young prophet is called. This servant of God is destined to spew harsh words and travel a hard road. "See, today, I appoint you over nations and kingdom, To pluck up and pull down. To destroy and overthrow. To build and to plant" (Jer. 1:10). Jeremiah was commissioned to confront Israel with their sin and brokenness, and break the news of the Babylonian captivity: The God of Israel says, "I will bring disaster to this place…they will eat the flesh of their sons…listen, you shepherds, it is your day to be slaughtered" (Jer. 19:6ff; 25:34). False prophets had declared that God would never let such a thing happen to his covenant people; the people welcomed them, and scorned the true prophet for bringing a message no one wanted to hear. Accused of cursing the temple, the very dwelling of God, Jeremiah was beaten and shackled in stocks just outside the city gates. Here he became the laughing-stock of everyone in the city. Tried and wearied, the prophet lamented his very birth. History would name him "the weeping prophet."

This passage is preceded by chapters that castigate the children of the covenant, while holding forth a sliver of hope for a remnant who obey Jeremiah's scandalous message, accept surrender, and willingly walk into Babylonian captivity. These would be restored. However, those who stayed in the holy city God would "make abhorrent before all kingdoms" and destroy by plague, famine, or the sword (24:10).

That God should give new hearts to the remnant and bring them home appears almost arbitrary. There is minimal support for the suggestion that God's choice here is a reward for listening to the prophet. No, it appears that God simply decides to maintain his covenant promises through them. Paradoxically, generations later, when deliverance comes and they are indeed free to return to Jerusalem, many of them determine to stay in Babylon. This is why Jews have both a Jerusalem and a Babylonian Talmud. Because people are people, I do not know of any day when God's people returned to him with their whole heart. Perhaps that time is yet to come.

> God, I resist the common interpretation that the way the prophets of Israel understood you is a typology of how you work with all nations. They understood themselves to be a theocracy, so all of history was in your hands. While I am not convinced of the intimacy between God and country that their interpretation suggests, I do pray that all peoples will return to you. Amen.

No Close-fistedness to a Buddha

Those who are generous are blessed, for they share their bread with the poor. Proverbs 22:9

Those blest with a generous heart give to the poor. It has always been that in giving we receive, and the joy received in giving makes the heart even more generous. Those who give to the poor are blessed with a generous heart. This is a natural outflow of understanding our interdependence with all people. We do not stand separate from them. We are them and they are us. In part, the blessing in giving is the peace that comes from trusting that we, in turn, will be the benefactors of benevolence in times of our own impoverishment: material or spiritual. There will always be others to stand with us. The many are the one. Our wealth rests in our interdependence. We live in a spirit of generosity because we can bank on the fact that in true community our withdrawals need never balance. This explains, in part, the refusal of Muslims to charge each other interest on borrowed money. The community or *ummah*, in line with Quranic teaching, holds a high standard of inner-faith support.

Siddhartha Guatama (b. 563 B.C.E.) eventually became the Buddha. He was born into one of the higher Hindu castes. His family had the money and education to propel him toward greatness. Much like the prosperity teachers in the Hebrew Scriptures, they chalked-up their fortune to God's good favor. A prophecy at his birth claimed that if he ever witnessed suffering he would become a great sage; but if he was protected from seeing the pain of life, as his parents hoped to accomplish, he would be a great king. When Siddhartha was 29 years old, the veil of protection was accidently removed. He was so shocked by the reality of suffering that he left his family to seek a way to alleviate humanity's suffering, and spent six years with monks who practiced hard core asceticism. But Siddhartha did not find contentment through fasting and other monastic traditions. Leaving that community helped him formulate a concept of the balanced life or Middle Path: Life is neither self-indulgence, nor is it living in extreme asceticism or poverty. This insight, plus the Four Noble Truths and Eight-Fold path, ushered Siddhartha into becoming the Buddha – a fully enlightened human being. For the remaining 45 years of his life, the Buddha taught the truths he learned. His compassionate mission was to help people learn how to cope with, if not escape, suffering. One truth he taught which is relevant to so many aspects of life was that "there is no close-fistedness to a Buddha." A truly enlightened person knows the freedom of open palms. As a matter of fact, our humanity is in our hands.

> *O God, grant your people of every faith and non-faith a desire to share and to experience the joy of giving. May that joy give us the freedom to open our hands even wider to those in need. Amen.*

No Longer Strangers

You are no longer strangers and sojourners, but fellow citizens with the saints and members of the household of God. Ephesians 2:19

He sat in the back row of the classroom, big, black, and bold enough to stare me down with his boredom. This guy had forgotten his past: blacks should not look a white man or woman in the eyes. That rule, of course, is a projection of the white man's inner darkness. Yet that projector turned on when those brown eyes glowered at me too strongly. I generally celebrate my students' liberation, yet I shudder before this fellow's audacity. Will he be the first to challenge the sacred order of my classroom with disruptive behavior? If I ask him to leave, might he challenge me? And how dare he fall asleep? I work hard to create an engaging atmosphere. Are his pupils dilated? What's he been smoking?

Already, I have made him the other, and we are strangers. I hate feeling this way. There is no peace. I am captive to the history that has shaped me. My fears squelch the freedom to relax, laugh, and go with the flow that I experience with his colleagues – both white and black. I assume I know his issues. It doesn't surprise me when he doesn't turn in assignments. Then things get complicated. Like any good professor, I must talk to him about his neglect. It is the proper, professional thing to do. He can no longer be the stranger. I must find that one kernel of truth somewhere in the mix of excuses that are sure to be told. He is part of this classroom, this household of assorted seekers. He deserves the right to a hearing. The Scriptures state: "He (Jesus) is our peace, who has made the two groups one and has destroyed the barrier, the dividing wall of hostility" (Eph. 2:14). Shouldn't I look at least a little bit like Jesus? He knew no strangers. There was no "other" to stare him down. He lifted everybody up. I am called to be "cross-eyed."

I get-up off my knees at the sound of knocking on my office door. I *want* to know his story. If only I had asked before. He is big, but he is not bored or belligerent. This poor young man is simply tired. That's all – just completely exhausted. In an attempt to support an aging mother and a growing child, he works forty hours a week. He goes to class all day, then sleeps a bit, then supervises the home-life for a few hours while studying in-between, and then hits the night shift! On occasion, he catches a wink in his car before class starts.

I could not hide the tears forming in my eyes. I never heard a more touching story of hope, discipline, and hard-work from the lips of a student. He believed in prayer, so we prayed. It was my fault that we had been strangers; but no longer.

Dear God, free me from those stereotypes, prejudices, and prideful thoughts that makes a man a stranger. Amen.

Overflow of the Altered Heart

And to the rest of you, brothers and sisters, never grow tired of doing good." 2 Thessalonians 3:13

Skeptics claim that as captives of our own self-centered struggle for survival we can never be truly altruistic. Some may be cynics who cannot escape their own bias. The fact is, good religion offers good reasons for doing good for goodness sake. The Hindu tradition offers four specific types of yoga (among other paths) to aid the journey toward God. The practice of yoga draws a person to the divine. The Hindu concept of karma (kama) yoga involves selfless service to others without concern for reward or consequence. The definition of yoga is to yoke or unite. The goal of every Hindu is to unite one's atman (self) with the Brahman (God). In fact, one's ignorance of his or her oneness with God leaves that person in a confounding state of sin or separation. One's dharma is to do good. There is a dharmic/karmic touch to the words of Jesus when he talks about giving to the poor: "Don't let the left hand know what the right hand is doing" (Matthew 6:3.)

Of course the cynic could say that yoga itself is selfishly motivated, because it offers the reward of finding true self in the Godself. The action cannot be separated from intention. There is warrant to that argument; yet the practitioner's intent is to know and love God, which requires losing the self in the fullness of God. Life in God flows with love and compassion because the creature has tapped into the streams of living water that course from the Creator's veins. A person fed through this intimate connection cannot help but fill another's cup. It is not disguised self-interest, but rather evidence of arrival at the crossroads of compassion where the hunger to help meets human need. That hunger is not a means of saving the species or accumulating spiritual merit. Rather, it is a true reflection of the heart of a God who never tires of doing good. Jesus said, "I am come that you might have life and that you would have life abundantly." It is our gratitude and trust in a God who gives "more than we could ever ask or think" that grants us freedom from self-protectionism and self-servitude. For the Christian, and many others who live in gratitude, altruism is the abundant overflow of a transformed heart.

> *"God of the weary heart" do not let me go. Do not let my questions defer compassion. Do not let my cynicism diminish my gratitude. Do not let a sometimes calloused heart hold back tender hands of service. Help me to yoke to the goodness of the Godhead. Amen.*

Paul and Prosperity Preaching

For the love of money is a root of all kinds of evil, and in their eagerness to be rich some have wandered away from the faith and pierced themselves with many pains. 1 Timothy 6:10

Does this sound like an old-time warning against the new day prosperity preaching? The other day I heard one such preacher share what he called "a sudden urging of the Spirit." The "urging" went like this: "God is telling me right now that He wants to cancel your credit card debt. God does not like debt and you do not need to be in debt. You may have hundreds or thousands of dollars on your credit card. God wants to release that debt today. God is telling me that if you will sow a $1,000 seed with your credit card, He will miraculously cancel all your debt. But you have to sow the seed immediately. Remember that delayed obedience is disobedience. Go to your phone right now, sow your seed and claim victory over that debt that Satan is forever holding over your head."

Paul's conclusion in verse ten is prefaced by "a word to the wise" (as my father use to say) about false teachers who "are depraved in mind and bereft of the truth, imagining that godliness is a means of gain" (I Tim. 6:5). I encourage all those who claim that material wealth stands as a witness of God's blessing, to read deeper than certain theological perspectives found within the Hebrew scriptures. Even their prophets challenged that theology. Then I would ask them to hear, with any ears that can hear, the teachings of Jesus and Paul, who continues: "There is great gain in godliness with contentment; for we brought nothing into the world, and we cannot take anything out of the world; but if we have food and clothing, with these we shall be content" (I Tim. 6:6-9).

Dear God, in this world that goes for the gold, help us not to be fooled. Amen.

Pauline Atonement Theology – Not Mine

> Brothers and sisters: When the fullness of time had come, God sent his Son, born of a woman, born under the law, to ransom those under the law, so that we might receive adoption as sons. As proof that you are sons, God sent the Spirit of his Son into our hearts, crying out, "Abba, Father!" So you are no longer a slave but a son, and if a son then also an heir, through God. *Galatians 4:4-7*

The moorings of Christian theology arise from the earthy consciousness of one person – the Apostle Paul. His experiences (and his interpretations of them) have become normative for the church. A tracker could trace Paul's theological journey back to the Jewish traditions that formed him; but in the wake of his conversion experience, Paul determined to "ride out of Dodge" as quickly as his hermeneutical horse could gallop. When the dust settled, and blinded eyes could see more clearly, he forged a new theology that related to, but was obviously distinguishable from, his traditional Jewish roots. Divine inspiration in Paul's life was siphoned through a filter of personality and historical experience. These stood together as the ground of his being that would erupt into a new creation. The Apostle's comprehension was conditioned by language and culture.

This is why Paul's language of atonement reflects a blend of law and love. He was attempting to communicate the good news to fellow citizens who were bound by their Jewish traditions. Even if Paul himself had a different frame of reference, he was limited to the language, stories, and images of his audience. Truth could not be conveyed in the abstract. Depictions of sacrifice and ransom were rampant in Jewish tradition, so Paul puts his picture of God's work within a framework his people can readily appreciate. Reared in the legalism of his day, the Apostle became a persecutor of those who strayed from allegiance to the culture's us/them, right/wrong distinctions. Yet as extreme as he was, his radical conversion transformed Paul to an equal extreme of love. In retrospect, his former condition must have felt like cold, harsh enslavement. It could not hold a candle to the warm, tender experience of being born a child of God. The spirit of Paul's God-relationship changed from that of a fearful son dutifully obeying his demanding father, to a child who longs to please a daddy who will never abandon him. His daddy's love is greater than the son's inability to live up to it.

I do not, as a Christian, feel compelled to use the atonement language of sacrifice and ransom that Paul had to use in order to effectively communicate the meaning of Jesus' death to the people of his time. The perfect sacrifice, lamb without blemish metaphor worked for Paul's culture, but it does not have to work for mine. I do not want to diminish the depth of human sin, the relational consequences of separation from God, nor the need to be salvaged from the wrecks of our lives. But I cannot accept Paul's interpretation of Jesus' death when he speaks about an angry God who demands a sacrifice (substitutionary atonement theory). Currently, Albelard's theory of the moral exemplar speaks to me. Of even greater interest is Rene Girard's understanding of Jesus' death as the quintessential example of rejection of vengeance and violence, issuing in God's validation of the voiceless victim.

> *God, it is frightening to be here, hanging out on this heretical limb. In that light, I really don't know how to pray. Should I confess my sin or ask for courage to continue stretching traditional boundaries? Dare I do both? Amen.*

Please, No Garlands Around My Neck

In that day the Lord of hosts will be a garland of glory, and a diadem of beauty, to the remnant of [God's] people; and a spirit of justice to the one who sits in judgment, and strength to those who turn back the battle at the gate. Isaiah 28:5-6

These verses follow on the heels of previous chapters that castigate nations who have treated Israel unkindly. Isaiah predicts the coming captivity in Babylon, but promises that Israel's enemies will "in that day" become God's whipping post. You simply do not mess with the covenant people and get away with it. The "spirit of justice" in today's text is good news for the surviving remnant, but big time bad news for the Babylonians. "That day" will be commemorated as a day of deliverance for the remnant, but Babylon will remember it as the day Israel's God unleashed vengeful terror upon their community. There may be times when a believer feels so battered by life that she longs for the day the enemy will get his just desserts; but this is not Jesus' style justice! I find no solace here. I am not drawn toward this kind of God.

Please God, don't put any garlands around my neck. Jesus is the only one who deserves the tribute as "a diadem of beauty." Amen.

Postscript:
The World Is Where You Sit

Warm sunshine streams through the kitchen windows. Spring can no longer hide her resurrection. The snow-crusted lawn is giving way to brilliant green, and robins are singing with winter's songbirds. A quiet solace settles upon my soul. There is nothing but nature; no one but Mel and a variety of birds, the boundless sky, and trees swaying effortlessly in the breeze. This is my world on a Saturday morning when life is slow and the air is sweet. Here I find sanctuary from the fast pace of "so much to do." It's a world where purity and innocence plays just outside my window. The world is where I sit.

Yet there are those look for the first signs of spring to break through the brown earth of window boxes, mounted on the front porches of their row homes, while a pigeon or two pecks away at morsels scattered beside an over-turned garbage can. A neighbor's angry voice screams obscenities at her spouse as a pusher makes his first deal on the corner of Parrish and Girard. The passerby lustfully flips the finger at a fine contoured figure who just wants to *be* – not gotten. Children run out from dilapidated buildings for a few swings of sidewalk jump rope, while older boys dodge honking cars during their game of stickball. There are no trees. Slabs of cement substitute for green grass, and a few common song sparrows join the cooing pigeons. Skyscrapers shadow the morning sun. Here, people sit on their porches Saturday after Saturday morning because they have nothing else in the world to do. Poverty rules, and innocence is lost out there beyond the chilled, concrete steps. The world is where they sit.

Every day, different people see a different world, experiencing unique realities. Each moment becomes a memory that structures the mind's convictions about life and one's core values, which vary with point of view. Things look different from the windows of a country home and an inner-city row house. Truths about trust, love, hope, God, nature, and humanity are relative to point of reference.

Why do we sit in different places? Is it destiny, fate, blessing, or curse? How is it that I happen to sit here, while you are over there? Did either of us deserve these stations? Does the Divine despair or delight over this dichotomy? Will our worlds ever meet? Do we have to stay where we sit?

Prayer, Buddha, and Jesus

"I believe that I shall see the goodness of the Lord in the land of the living. Wait for the Lord; be strong, and let your heart take courage; wait for the Lord!" *Psalms* 27:13-14

I have often struggled with waiting in relation to prayer. I have preached countless sermons about the reasons for unanswered prayer, ranging from the believer's sin, lack of faith, and anxiety, to the various lessons God might want to teach us. Yet I question whether transformation is a direct consequence of prayer as much as a determined exercise of the mind. I believe prayer fertilizes growth of character and the process of becoming a more spirit-filled person. It is a timed-release feeding of the mind, which serves as a reminder of whose we are, and how we want to live. Other believers join in these hope-filled petitions and encourage accountability. Eventually, we become the product of our aspirations; for whatever one thinks, one becomes.

My thoughts about prayer are perhaps more suitably aligned with the Buddhist perspective. Obviously, though, this is problematic because the Buddha approached life from an atheistic perspective of "be a lamp unto yourself." From a traditional Christian point of view, conversion is the work of God's forgiving and reconciling Spirit through the efficacious act of Christ's death on the cross, and resurrection. Belief in these dogmas bridges the great divide our sins have caused between us and God. For the Buddhist, however, sins are signs of our ignorance. They are the consequences of misdirected desires, and they twist our relationships with others. They can be redirected and reeducated, however, through meditation and choosing to live in the manner of the Eight-fold Path. I find some intriguing similarities between the

Christian's "fruit of the Spirit" and the Buddhist Eight-fold Path. The Christian claims that one cannot bear fruit without the Spirit of God, while the Buddhist believes that the will to do what is right already resides within us. The practice for both traditions, however, is living a less ego-centered, more compassionate life, with prayer and meditation integral parts of the transformation process for both religions. I am deeply indebted to the Buddhist perspective of staying in one place, losing self in the moment, and finding peace in emptiness. Yet I am hesitant to shift to Buddhism because it does not recognize the concept of a relational God who is at work in the believer's heart.

On the other hand, when Christians confront unanswered prayer they often let God off the hook with statements like "in his time," or "God knows best," or "have faith and patience." These catch-phrases are attempts to ease the *dis-ease*, fill the empty silence, or placate God. Unanswered prayer positions us before the bedside of a sleeping deity. Why do we have to scream so loudly above his slumbering snores just to hear a timely response? Call it lack of faith, the futility of a sinful perspective, or faltering courage – put whatever label upon it that fits your fancy; for me, this shouting and waiting seems less than redemptive.

> *Well, God, I guess you heard the disenchantment in that reflection. It would be proper, I suppose to pray with the composer, "Teach me Lord to wait, down on my knees; 'til in your own good time, you answer my pleas." Right now, I'm not in the placating mood. It's your turn to wait. I pray that you will. Amen.*

Postscript
In Gratitude to Buddhism

Running on Empty

Milky-white clouds filter the four o'clock sun.
Warmth falls soft as a grandmother's lingering embrace.
It blankets body and soul.
This country road is covered in quietness
But for the meadowlark call and the locust chirp.
My mind wanders beyond nature's sanctuary
To what could or should be.
A pinkish clover peeks through the roadside grass.
She whispers, "Stay with what is."
In mindless obedience my gaze turns downward.
The myriad of cracks in the asphalt morph into
Patterned markings of a box turtle.
As it should be - I am losing my mind.
The morning glory shouts a full-faced praise

For the silence of my emptiness.
I am nowhere, but here.
I know nothing, but everything.
I am empty, but full.
Grandmother smiles.

Empty and Free (2006)

It came so gently to the silent spot
Mystery took me where mind could not
When nothingness crept through my door
And I wasn't, where I was before.

It summoned me softly to a place of peace
Where the emptiness of life's sweet release
Filled the void with the great Thou Art
And whisked the I from this willing heart

T' was not me on that far off shore
Yet who else was, that the raft did bore?
I can't find me, but I know I'm found
Somewhere free, twixt sky and ground.

Prayers for Healing and Puzzlement

But now more than ever the word about Jesus spread abroad; many crowds would gather to hear him and to be cured of their diseases. But he would withdraw to deserted places and pray." Luke 5:15-16

Jesus did it. His disciples did it. And he said we could do it. Benny Hinn does it. Yet, in my hundreds of bedside prayers for healing, I cannot with certainty claim one hit. Sure, there have been sighs of relief and smiles of comfort; but a straight-up, unquestionable cure as a consequence of a pastoral prayer – not one. Maybe I didn't pray long enough? Shout loud enough? Proclaim faith strongly enough? But as the years progressed, a part of me said 'I've had enough." Prayers for healing had begun to sound like best-wishes for the bedridden. There were times in my ministry when I had mustered greater faith. But after years of being applauded by my congregants for knowing just what to say and how to pray, but seeing no lasting physical changes, I concluded those kinds of prayers were not my expertise. The frustration of this aspect of ministry contributed to my exit.

I find it baffling, during worship service joys and concerns, to hear my current pastor praise God for answered prayer on behalf of someone who is feeling better, when others are feeling worse. The dozens of unanswered petitions are never acknowledged. My pastor works his ministry with compassion and hope. I serve the former, but have to stretch for the latter. Although periodically the miraculous does occur, and praise is appropriate, for the most part life just seems to happen, and the body takes the consequences.

In spite of my ambivalence, I now fast and pray for the healing of my wife, who has been battling debilitating chronic pain for six years. I'd like to say I am doing this because I sincerely believe she will get better; it would be more honest to say I am doing it because I think I should. Douglas Steer, in his book *Dimensions of Prayer*, confronts the intent of the petitioner: *Is the person only out to get safely through the extremity or is he prepared, impelled by the extremity, to turn around to discover and move on into a new dimension of life?* Well, the present dimension doesn't feel so good. We have both grown tired of praying "whatever it takes for wholeness' sake," or to be able just to "move on." I do not want anything I am doing or not doing to be a barrier to my wife's wholeness, so I'll keep trying. Yet, in the back of my mind I wonder what concentrated prayer can do, when years of prayer have already been offered on her behalf. Quite honestly, even if she did get well I would not be quick to call it an answer to prayer. Maybe she simply . . . I don't know . . . got well? I grow desperate before the mystery of life and prayer.

> *I suspect, O God, that prayer is a pronouncement of hope; a plea for an experiential awareness of your presence; a petition that is offered with varying degrees of expectation. Lately, God, I've been deficient in each of these aspects of prayer. I desired more, was more disciplined in the past, and determined to close the door on doubt, but it seems like "the prayer of this (the) righteous man availeth" little (James 5:16). Perhaps, I am not righteous enough? What more can I say? What more can I pray? Amen.*

Postscript: In Love and Suffering

"I Do"

Dear Joan,

It has been a difficult year, but it has been a great year for love. The deep, abiding warmth we felt in those moments when we simply held each other is so much more memorable than the pain that drew us close. Your embrace is healing. Many years ago, I promised to love and cherish you in sickness and health, but little did I know then that now, in the midst of this present affliction, I would love you more. You both succor and seduce me with your strength. Your spirit of determined optimism is rarely compromised by the duration of pain, and even when the dragon wins, the battle was fought with the kind of integrity that would make any façade of victory disingenuous. You are a picture of beauty to me whether your face be brimmed with a smile or moistened with tears. Let's grow old together, my dear. Sure, I know we are merely in the middle of a love of lengthening years, but in this moment, at this time our bodies seem to have betrayed the reality of our youthful minds. That's alright. Even if this season sees no spring we have a scent of love that wafts from sources unseen. The lotus blossom is our sister. Let these fractured bodies that hold us down be the fertile soil of uplifted souls. Acting our age will be the wisdom of being grounded in an ageless love. Maybe this is what Jesus means when he says, "I am come that you might have life and have it abundantly." If these words express truth, then old love can be the most complete love. You know, it might well be true; for just when I think I could not love you more – I do. May this 53rd year be filled with abundance!

    All my love, Mel

    (February 12, 2008)

Roots and the River: Do Not Fear

But blessed is the one who trusts in Me alone; the Eternal will be his confidence. He is like a tree planted by water, sending out its roots beside the stream. It does not fear the heat or even drought. Its leaves stay green and its fruit is dependable, no matter what it faces. *Jeremiah 17:7-8*

Rich with poetic metaphor, this verse overflows with waters of wisdom. It paints the place where I used to be, and in some ways aspire to be again. Yet one can never step into the same river twice. By the time the next foot touches bottom the rushing current has transformed the stream. All things change. There is a beautiful story called "The River and the Clouds," written by Tich Nhat Hanh, which captures the essence of Buddha's teachings about the Four Noble Truths. In this story, the once joyful river begins to obsess over the fact that she cannot possess any of the clouds that are reflected upon her waters. Her desire to hold on to something that is impermanent and ever-changing brings her misery. Eventually she reaches such depths of despair that she wants to take her life. But she is finally saved by her willingness to let go of her desire, and appreciate the wonder of the clouds coming and passing. She no longer has to cling, possess, manipulate, and control. The river basks in the beauty each moment brings. She is free to embrace change, and released from fear of the future.

Lately, I have attempted to live by drawing from old and drying wells rather than dipping in fresh rivers. I try to conjure trickles of bygone days, when I could be bathing daily in the living waters the Deity provides. My roots are dry, my leaves are withered, and my fruit unripe. I need to step into the river once again and trust the current of the Spirit.

> *God, I have no fresh words to offer. You've heard them all before. Futility falls from my lips. Amen.*

Postscript: Do Not Fear
(A Bit Of Buddhist Perspective)

My eyes wide open to my death as they fasten upon the reflection of an aging face, filtered through the hue of a computer screen. That flint-faced stranger seems determined to call me friend. Whitened beard, wrinkled brow, tilted bifocals form-fitted to a once broken nose – they all beg for acceptance. But I peer back in disbelief. That face is the unclaimed freight of a future yet to be. How dare it demand an acceptance kiss from the present! That worn old countenance does no justice to the adolescent spirit of adventure that even now flushes my veins with a life-affirming rush.

A slight grin forms on the lips of the other, as if to say, "do not fear; the time of your life is now."

The waves crash upon the shore. Like the sandpipers scampering just beyond water's edge, I scurry to higher ground. "Don't get those new sneakers wet" warns the mother within me. Who is the *me* I say I am? Who is the wave? I feel her as female. Does she claim a self? Does she know her form is conditioned by forces beyond her lovely contoured crest: an inevitable expression of the slope of the shore and the sea flowing back to herself? No, no self is found within the flaunting of her form. In the blink of an eye she is nothing more than foam percolating into the sands. All things pass. The brisk November breeze whispers, "do not fear; her time is now."

There is a *now* in every time. Every time is the eternity we share. Am I the foam that dissipates upon the shore, leaving no trace upon the sand? My feet imprint the sand. Thousands of particles sink under the pressure of every footstep. The way I walk upon the sands of time in this life make eternal impressions in the lives of others. We share a future.

My eyes wide open to the death of me, I see my reflection in the life of you. Hold my hand. Our time is now. Do not fear.

Seeds of Justice and the Powers That Be

Again I saw all the oppressions that are practiced under the sun. Look, the tears of the oppressed -- with no one to comfort them! On the side of their oppressors there was power -- with no one to comfort them. Ecclesiastes 4:1

The preacher in this passage speaks to us today, for our experience is no different than his, as he laments life through a lens of death. All around him, those in positions of privilege and power were slowly squeezing the last breath from the poor. In light of the Hebrew belief in Sheol – mysterious nether-land of meaningless existence – for the writer to say that being dead in Sheol is better than being born expresses a truly grim hopelessness.

Walter Wink, in his book *Powers That Be* notes that "evil is not just personal, but structural and spiritual." Power is on the side of the oppressor, and there is no one under the heavens to dry the victims' tear-stained cheeks. Will the powers that be, always be in power? Probably so. Corruption bakes the pie and slices the portions. On the other hand, there will always be small pockets of life where the voice of the victim will scandalize the system and scatter the princes of power from their citadels. Where the proletariat, like a tiny seed, is fertilized and transformed, the kingdom of God will spring into flower. The lamenter's warning, like his lasting hope, rests in a final statement of faith that "the beginning of wisdom is the fear (reverence and awe) of the Lord."

O Lord of Life, images of suffering and death surround me. It can sink to the depths of my soul and shatter my sense of hope. Help me to hold on and once again dirty my hands for the sake of your kingdom come. Amen.

The Shona and the Seventh Year

But the seventh year you shall let it rest and lie fallow, so that the poor of your people may eat; and what they leave the wild animals may eat. You shall do the same with your vineyard, and with your olive orchard. Exodus 23:11

The Shona tribe in Zimbabwe, as I'm sure do other African cultures, practice the kind of concern for the poor that captures the spirit of today's passage. The farmers do not build fences to keep out either four- or two-footed creatures. In fact, the fields are open to those who have need. If a hungry person walks by a crop of corn he is free to pick and eat what he needs for that day. In fact, it is assumed that he will shuck a few ears, sit down, relax, and light a fire. The rising smoke will signal the poor man's gratitude for the farmer's generosity. Shona believe that any farmer who builds fences around his property will find misfortune just around the corner. May such freedom fill my spirit each year – not merely every seventh.

O Spirit of Africa, break down the fences I have constructed around what I have claimed to be mine. May smoke frequently rise from the fields that you have entrusted to me. Amen.

Sinister Canopy of Nationalism

Sing aloud, O daughter of Zion; shout, O Israel! Rejoice and exult with all your heart, O daughter of Jerusalem! The Lord has taken away the judgments against you, [The Lord] has turned away your enemies. The king of Israel, the Lord, is in your midst; you shall fear disaster no more."
Zephaniah 3:14-15

Of course, this is a word for a people living under a theocracy. They are convinced that through them and their nation, God is achieving a plan of salvation. Is this a myopic focus on a drop of water, misperceived to be the entire ocean rippling with the ebbs and tides of the consequences of their decisions? Is this an exaggerated account of the divine-human dialogue? Or is it the unique expression of a group of people so incredibly connected to their Creator that they shared the intimacy of a son or daughter with the High God, One would hold them accountable to their mission to bring *shalom* to the global village?

That covenantal intimacy has captured the soul of my own nation. Many are convinced that *we* are the people of God; as though we are the theocracy that God chastises with disaster, disciplines with suffering, and draws with divine love. They would swear under the flag, hand upon Bible, that the United States of America is the beacon on a hill. We are sanctioned by divine dictate to be the New Israel, called to manifest the blessing for the world that was promised to Abraham, our father of faith.

I think both the old and "new" Israel have flashes of genuine human goodness, as well as the shortcomings of ethnocentrism, nationalism, and flagrant pathology that corrupts all peoples. I struggle with the idea that our scriptures were inspired by a sacred reality. Have we merely projected a sacred radiance upon a secular, contrived story?

> God, kingdoms come and go. I know that my tradition claims to see your story of salvation history through our sacred script. I also know that in my cynicism towards that claim I cannot come to you on bended knee and unwavering belief. I don't know just how you will attend to my lack of reverence. So, I say a frightful, "Amen."

Postscript

Then I Saw Her Face: Facades of Faith in the U.S.

Davey Jones died recently, that boyish-faced British star of the famous band, The Monkeys. But the song that catapulted them to the top of the charts, "I'm a Believer," will live on as a rock and roll legacy. Sing the first phrase of the chorus, "Then I saw her face," and others quickly chime in with the second: "Now I'm a believer!" It captures that moment of innocent attraction that leaves the admirer helplessly lost in the euphoria of an impassioned first glance, which can see not the slightest blemish. The one beheld is granted license as spacious as the sky. To acknowledge a third-party's critique would be to kill the dream. Any crack on the face of the vision would spur disbelief. The threat of truth requires the absence of judgment, and anyone raising questions is considered hostile, heretical, and ungrateful – an enemy of the Holy Alliance.

So it is that many who sing "God Bless America" have difficulty believing we are anything but that beacon on a hill, destined by the Divine to rescue those who are drowning in the high seas of personal sin or undemocratic regimes. This belief struck a chord with Americans during our formative years. It has been deeply ingrained into the psyche of the citizenry. To see our nation in any other light is disturbing. It is hard to leave home. The conviction that God has blessed America carries such sacred sanction that inquiry and protest automatically become an ungrateful challenge to the state; even more – a disgrace to The Almighty. This union of God and country is grounded in sermons like John Winthrop's 1630 proclamation to The Massachusetts Bay Colony. He entitled his sermon "A Modell of Christian Charity:"

> For wee must consider that wee being a city upon a hill, the eies of all people are upon us; so that if wee deal falsely with our God in this worke wee have undertaken and soe cause him to withdraw his present help from us, we shall be made a story and a by-wordthrough the world, wee shall open the mouths of enemies to speak evil of the ways of god and all professours for God's sake.

We found ourselves immersed in this story for centuries after. As Larry Witham notes in his book, *A City Upon A Hill*, from the days of Winthrop, when "published sermons outnumbered almanacs, newspapers, and political pamphlets by four to one" to the present, preachers have pounded pulpits and hounded parishioners with sermons that paint the colonists as the New Israel entering the Promised Land destined to them by God. Like ancient Israel, divine sanction became a license to kill, and in the case of the U.S., to colonize regardless of costs to the lives of Native Americans and enslaved blacks. Here were holocausts perpetrated under the guise of God's manifest destiny for a nation motivated by an individualistic, gold rush mentality at the horrific expense of others. She claimed that her pursuits and pleasures were signs of divine blessing. We claim that still. Driven by the myth that God is on our side and the other is simply in the way of the right, we have confused materialism with blessing and militarism with peace. The United States, compelled by her sense of entitlement, has gone into all the world to take what resources it can glean from other countries, in order to sustain a standard of living claimed as God's bounty.

Could it be that God has not blessed us at all, that we have simply gone out and grabbed what we could, and then stamped "In God We Trust" on our currency? Our over-indulgence has become a significant part of our national interest that warrants military protection. It is a far stretch to claim that in contrast to all other countries the United States stands as the epitome of the Kingdom of God come to earth, particularly if the Kingdom of God is most brilliantly reflected in the life and teachings of Jesus Christ. This man, who lived under the politics of an oppressive military regime, goes to his death with neither the spirit of vengeance nor the sword of violence. And he invites others to "Take-up your cross and follow me." When the blinders are removed, we can look into the mirror and see nationalism just a scratch beneath the façade of faith. In our eagerness to invoke divine approval upon past and present policies that stray far from the ethics of Jesus, we dance with the devil of denial, all the while flaunting a self-righteous swagger that other countries abhor.

Hypocrisy abounds. In his *Political Observations* of 1795, James Madison warns: *Of all the enemies to public liberty war is, perhaps, the most to be dreaded because it comprises and develops the germ of every other. War is the parent of armies; from these proceed debts and taxes ... known instruments for bringing the many under the domination of the few.... No nation could preserve its freedom in the midst of continual warfare.*

Prophetic words, indeed! Our defense spending continues to soar beyond $900 billion, and the defense budget remains sacrosanct even to a liberal leadership. These priorities rise to the top while programs related to poverty are downsized. The budget is a statement of morality, and it stands as a clear indicator of to what or to whom we bow. In 1961, nearing the end of his days in the Whitehouse, President Dwight Eisenhower gave this sobering caution to his country: "We must guard against unwarranted influence, whether sought or unsought, by the military-industrial complex. The potential for the disastrous rise of misplaced power exists and will persist."

The United States paints her face with the concealer and mascara of peace, while producing more weapons of destruction than any other country in the world. From 2003 to 2010, the U.S. cornered $170,764 billion, or 39%, of the arms sales market around the globe. Russia scored a distant second of 18%. Many people of faith, myself included, lament the number of abortions done in our country, yet paradoxically there is not a loud cry from the pro-life sector against the manufacturing of weapons that wound and kill thousands each year. A good number of these sincere people of faith actually concur with large defense expenditures. Such inconsistency in their pro-life position seems hypocritical. Thousands each year are killed, including babies and children, with additional millions of innocent people displaced or dying from the ravages of wars fought with weapons America manufactured. "God is on our side, so our might makes right" is not a statement of faith but a fear-based projection of the anxiety of self-survival, aroused in part by the "unwarranted influence of the military industrial complex." Our economy thrives on weapons of war. Like ancient Israel, we bow to the Baal of fertility: whatever makes the grass green, whatever makes the economy grow.

It is doubtful that Jesus could sanction our hawkish obsessions any more than he sanctioned the Zealots or the Romans, in the era of the Pax Romana. Jesus wept over a Jerusalem still swayed by the myth that

God delivers through vengeance and violence. Obviously, Jesus had not come to deliver that kind of messiah. I think he still weeps, because his world still believes the myth. We dare not call ourselves Christian or Christ-like under this light of truth. The 1976 aspiring Presidential candidate, Jimmy Carter, challenged our hypocrisy: "We can't have it both ways. We can't be both the world's leading champion of peace and the world's leading supplier of arms."

"Then I saw her face; now I'm a believer!" Yes, it's a lovely fantasy. But unquestioned allegiance needs the freedom of critique, doubt, and disbelief. There is a crack in the vision of nationalism and civil religion, and it looks like a cross.

Taming the Tongue

Let your speech always be gracious, seasoned with salt, so that you may know how you ought to answer everyone.
Proverbs 24:13-14

From the Psalmist's perspective, the words in our mouths are formed by the meditation of our hearts (Ps. 19:14). Jesus affirmed this upon his declaration that it is not that which comes from outside of ourselves that defiles us, but the things that stir from within the depths of our being (Mark 7:20). In that light, whenever the words on the tip of my tongue are not gracious I pause, for the cause may not lie in the external exigencies, but in my own fermenting unresolved anxiety, anger, or jealousy. Whenever I fail to favor friends or enemies with words that reflect salt's healing and preserving qualities, I know that the sin lies within me. Best that I shut up, sit down, listen, and look for how the Spirit wishes to enlighten my darkness. Only then will my words be tastefully seasoned.

I am disturbed by what appears to be a progressive lack of gracious speech in our society. In fact, there seems to be a groundswell of acceptance of language that demeans people. Sadly, this language – and the attitude behind it – is on display not only on late night shows like Howard Stern or Jerry Springer; we hear it also at work, at home, in the political arena, and even on Christian talk shows. We have forgotten to take James 3:5-8 seriously:

> So too the tongue is a small part of the body, yet it has great pretensions. Think how small a flame sets a huge forest ablaze. And the tongue is a fire! The tongue represents the world of wrongdoing among the parts of our bodies, that pollutes the entire body and sets fire to the course of human existence and is set

on fire by hell. For every kind of animal, bird, reptile, and sea creature is subdued and has been subdued by humankind. But no human can subdue the tongue; it is a restless evil, full of deadly poison.

This sin will strip us of our dignity, and the love we need for building healthy relationships. Our entire society will suffer demise.

> *Jesus, words do not come out of nowhere. They are the language of the soul. Keep my very being within the benevolence of your heart, so that my words will be flavored by your life-giving Spirit. Amen.*

Teach Me to Pray, Dad

Brothers and sisters, do not be weary in doing what is right.
II Thessalonians 3:13

Today, somewhere between New Orleans and Orlando, he called. I basked beneath a bright late-afternoon sky. Regardless of the earthly hour, this call was on *kairos* time. That's the classical *koine* Greek term used in the Bible to designate the grace of God's timing: a "could not have been better" kind of timing. How fitting for a wearying veteran of faith, whose faltering steps have frequently found him hapless in prayer. On the road with his band, my son continued, while the other guys listened in. He talked to me on the phone about a lot of things, but the one thing he said for which I have waited so long (so long in fact, that I felt foolish in my waiting) was this.

The comment sprang from a conversation regarding Toby's desire to still his spirit in the midst of some heavy decisions he and his wife were making about starting a family: "I have some really good friends who practice Transcendental Meditation. It helps them a lot." I mentioned that only an hour ago in my Introduction to Religion class we discussed the Buddhist goal of extinguishing desire through meditation. And last week a Zen Buddhist spoke to my Comparative Religion class about TM. I was about to say that I myself was considering the Zen approach, when Toby said, "But the thing I can't get into is that the Eastern religious adherents don't believe there is a metaphysical Reality beyond themselves. The God piece is missing. I don't know, Dad, but I sort of like the idea of someone being out there. It's comforting to believe that it's not all about me, or up to me."

I promptly squelched my words, as Toby continued. "So, I really want to know how to pray, Dad. When I get back, I want you to teach me how to pray."

For years, I practiced every type of prayer on the list to show my love for and find favor with God. Now I don't find much meaning in any of those approaches. In recent years, the best prayer I could do for my boys has been something like: "God, since I don't even know how to think about you, I cannot ask that my boys have an understanding of You that looks like mine — so just bring them closer to You and help them to live more like Jesus." That's it. That's all I have been requesting lately. Now there actually appears to be some movement in that direction.

Toby's new initiative seems so ironic. I am elated by it. Yet I am humbled, if not cowered, by the momentous task that lies before one who at this point in his sojourn feels he has so little to offer. Yet, when a son asks his father, "Father, teach me to pray," that father does not send him elsewhere. Obviously, since I have lived with integrity before him for 32 years, he sees something now that still speaks wholeness to him. But I feel so broken.

When I told my wife about this conversation, she too rejoiced. She then added, as one who has battled chronic pain from Lyme disease for more than six years, "Today, I asked God to give me just two hours, only two hours of pain free living, so I could teach and really be there without weariness. But nothing happened, Mel. Nothing happened. For years I have prayed. Nothing ever happens. I just don't know what I believe about prayer."

How in the world can God use two such broken vessels? Our treasured libations of wisdom have long since been poured out and have seeped into the soil. Shards from the broken vessels that poured them litter the ground. Yet somebody still believes these fallow fields are fertile. Can this father still teach his son to pray? Are we on *kairos* time? Somewhere between now and then, may God help us!

> *In the depths of doubt, I shudder at the thought of not being able to pass on the belief and beneficence of prayer to my sons, my grandsons, and granddaughters. May God help us! Amen.*

Postscript: Remember My Sons (2001)

Reach back, my sons and remember.
When you feel alone in this world, remember
- the many times you heard, "I love you"
- the hundreds of hours you lay so close to our breasts that our heartbeats became one
- the nighttime stories and the sheets being drawn snuggly around you
- the countless hours we stood on the side-lines simply watching you play
-backpacking on the trail, out of sight, but knowing we were somewhere behind you

Reach back, my sons and remember,
When the challenge of a new risk calls you, remember
-the first steps taken as you toddled into our arms

-waving goodbye in the darkness as the school bus drove away
-diving off the rocks at the Haystacks and repelling over the cliffs
-your first weekend at college
-family service projects

Reach back, my sons, and remember,
When difficult decisions confront you, remember
-life is never about only you
-the wisdom of our words and ways
-the love of God for you and the call to love even your enemies
-your own strength of character
-your heart must feel at home with your choice

Reach back, my sons, and remember,
When success taps you on the shoulder, remember
-you did, but you didn't do it on your own
-the attitude of gratitude
-the people who helped you and the experiences that formed you
-the steps you took to get there
-the failure at success is the one who forgets those in need around him

Reach back, my sons, and remember,
When life gets you down, remember
-the warmth of welcoming arms
-the dog of our dreams
-our family meetings and arguments over things that didn't matter
-vacationing in St. John
-your mother's smile

Reach back, my sons, remember
Tomorrow's hope is rooted in the memories of yesterday.

The Beginning of Strife

The beginning of strife is like letting out water; so stop before the quarrel breaks out. Proverbs 17:14

I spent countless hours of my childhood in the stream that flowed through our yard. It became a playground of exploration and discovery. I turned over rocks to catch scooting crayfish or slippery salamanders. I set my father's empty paint buckets downstream to trap the minnows that scurried from feet strategically splashing every upstream hiding place. The largest chub was a prize worth the envy of neighborhood boys. Nothing, however, compared to the capture of a water snake. This act of bravery became the proof that a barrier of boyhood fear had been broken. A snake can't bite when held just behind its head. As it helplessly writhes its body around your arm, the demon is defeated.

Anger can be an inner snake-demon that seems impossible to conquer. For whatever reason, some of us struggle with that monster, that grows bigger with every offense. Fortunately, some excellent books have been written about anger management in recent years; but for many it takes years of practice to gain the skill to use anger constructively and creatively in relationships. For those of us who grew up witnessing less than ideal models of anger, the emotion usually provokes either the silence of resentment, or a reckless wave of raging destruction.

The boys in the stream scoured the streambed for the biggest rocks to begin the process of building a dam worthy of bragging rights. The gaps between those behemoths that took two to carry, they patched with smaller stones. Like thick icing on a mother's cake, they plastered a mixture of mud and grass to fortify the dam's exterior wall. The waters rose. The beaver burned with envy.

But beware – rising waters cannot be contained, only controlled. An escape mechanism must relieve the pressure that builds behind the walls. The author of Proverbs 17:14 appears to have determined that the slightest leak will lead to a devastating rush of raging water: his metaphor for contagious emotional release that leads to a fight. Paul's *be angry, but do not sin* is not celebrated in this Proverb, where to let anything out is to let it *all* out. Much better, I believe, to take the wisdom of modern-day authors. Open a safety-valve so the truth of your anger will be spoken in love. If measured by love, it can be received. The relationship stays fertile.

> *Loving God, you long for us to live in harmonious relationships with others. Grant us the wisdom to know the physical signs of anger's early stages, so that we can find healthy outlets for its expression. Do not let us simply plug up holes and quietly deny and suppress the truth of our emotions. Release us, as well, from the overwhelming rushes of anger that drown the hopes of being heard. Amen.*

The Foul Beneath Our Feet

Is it not enough for you to feed on the good pasture, but you must tread down with your feet the rest of your pasture? When you drink of clear water, must you foul the rest with your feet? Ezekiel 34:18

Through this incredibly imaginative metaphor of injustice, Ezekiel castigates his elitist audience who consumes at the expense of the poor. He describes arrogant hearts characterized by relentless, materialistic pursuits that carelessly devastate creation. His metaphor transports us directly to the hardcore reality of modern humanity. Our footprints have hardened the soul of the earth. We have stripped her resources and walked away, heavy pockets torn with the weight our obsession for more. Our lumbering steps pound the globe's green pastures into infertility. Our world's waters have been polluted by feet chase luxury. We have not loved God's creation. Our corporate ego stands as the number-one enemy of our ecosystem, and the foul stench of death rests beneath our feet. And still, some of us deny our culpability.

God forgive us for the destructive domination we have wrought upon Your creation. Give us the courage to face our personal and corporate demons of extravagance. Help us to repent, not simply with our words, but with our ways. Grant us the fortitude to turn around, make an about-face, and partner as co-creators of life on this small piece of the cosmos you have dedicated to our stewardship. Help me to be conscious of those times when my wants become my needs and I become an agent of destruction rather than an ambassador of new creation. Amen.

The Narrow Path of Love

Enter through the narrow gate. For wide is the gate and broad is the road that leads to destruction, and many enter through it. But small is the gate and narrow the road that leads to life, and only a few find it. Matthew 7:13-14

Centuries of interpretation have strewn the path of right-living with the stumbling stones of legalism: a multitude of maxims concerning do's and don'ts that only a few pious and prideful could obey. Jesus opposed this hypocritical view of life in this passage. Jesus' narrow way was less traveled, but not because it was laden with legalisms defining who is "in" and who is "out." But as the Christian centuries progressed, ecclesiastical bodies added the specific steps they considered necessary to reach God's kingdom. These steps were meant to provide assurance of salvation. By the time Martin Luther came to the fore in Christian history, the Church had delineated confession, pilgrimages to holy places, baptism, indulgences, the adoration of relics, numerous additional rituals, and complete obedience to the authorities, as those "fruits" of righteousness preparing the way for eternal security.

Reformists in the Protestant traditions rightfully rebelled against the hypocrisy of their predecessors, but could not resist the temptation to set up their own standards. Anabaptists did the same. The legalisms they propounded maintained the distinctiveness that separated their group from all others. They all shared a spirit of superiority, along with denial of their shadow-side that compelled them to project evil upon the others without confronting their own sinfulness. Even as they narrowed their views to a "my way or the highway" mentality, they broadened the road of self-righteous malevolence toward others, directly opposed to the way of Jesus.

How do we enter through the narrow gate? Jesus offers us the key: "So in everything, do to others what you would have them do to you, for this sums up the Law and the Prophets." We enter in a fashion that respects the integrity of personhood: with the recognition that we are both saint and sinner; in a humbled spirit of truth that does not give us the freedom to point fingers and forget our shadow-side; in a love for others that refuses to label another as the stranger. This narrow way is hard because it insists that I recognize what I share in common with my enemy. It requires that I build relationships and seek reconciliation, demonstrating that mercy trumps judgmentalism. It was this commitment that compelled Martin Luther King, Jr. to preach that the oppressors were as oppressed as their victims.

In reality, it is so much easier to live by legalisms than to be bound by love. Yet it is in the narrows of love that life is broadened and truth deepened. The depths of love the most frightening lands to traverse. There the Spirit thrusts the believer into the far country where vulnerability, honesty, and openness fills the hearts of those who truly draw near to God. Relatively few follow this path. It is in this light that Jesus prefaces the Sermon on the Mount (Matthew 5:20) with, "Your righteousness must exceed that of the Scribes and Pharisees." He is not introducing a new legal system, but extending the boundaries of love.

> *Dear Jesus, let me walk upon the narrow path of love, so that I might find the life and be an ambassador of reconciliation and life to others. Amen.*

The News Is Not Good[2]

Accept, O Lord, the willing tribute of my lips, and teach me your judgment. My life is always in my hand, yet I do not forget your law. Psalm 119:108-109

Determined to believe again, I dutifully read the daily scripture lesson from Sojourners. Their persistent activism is grounded in a radical, evangelical interpretation of the sacred text. I barely believe, but their consistent witness keeps me clinging to the Vine. My head shakes with pathetic embarrassment over the thoughts that flood my mind when I read this verse. Damn it, I want to draw close, but instead of offering tribute I take God to task for insufficient revelation. I push God away. If the eternal destiny of those whom God wills "that not one would perish" is at stake, why would Jesus, God incarnate, be given a mere three-year stint on this earth? It seems so unjust to come just once, to one people, one particular culture, and assume they would be able to communicate effectively God's "Good News" to clans and cultures around the globe. That is not good judgment! God must be great beyond the Jesus whom Christianity claims is the only way to God – great enough to draw people of other cultures and religions. If not, then neither God nor the news is good!

I pray, O God, that this new sojourn into these Scriptures will ultimately be a story of good news. Amen.

---

[2] **(This was the first entry of Advent 2010, the date I started this devotional journey.)**

The Way

Jesus said to him, "I am the way, and the truth, and the life. No one comes to [God] except through me. If you know me, you will know my [Lord] also. From now on you do know [the Lord] and have seen [God]." John 14:6-7

"You see now, that bugs me," retorted my Universalist Unitarian friend. "Christians have always used that verse as an instrument of exclusivism. It creates a 'we're in, you're out' scenario. But doesn't it simply mean that the way to know God is to live and love like Jesus?"

I wonder if he's right. Does this preparation period of Advent suggest that if I prepare a place for Jesus in my life, God will be preparing an eternal reality for me? Must Jesus be God Incarnate in the flesh? Wasn't that church council in the A.D. 300's where fellow Christians screamed "heretic" in the faces of those who believed Jesus to be of similar substance but not the same essence as God, a bit over the top? Or should we take it with great seriousness that the majority considered this doctrine to be vital to Emmanuel (God with us)? If I can believe "of similar substance," but struggle with "of the same essence," is there no place for me? I know the spirit of Jesus. I attempt to follow Paul "the more excellent way" of love that Paul sets before us in I Corinthians 13; however, unlike Paul, I question the incarnation. If I do not believe that Jesus is God, am I disqualified from the Father's plan of salvation?

Joseph Runzo argues in his article "Secular Rights and Religious Responsibilities" that the greatest gift religion brings to ethics is not the mere protection of rights, which can be at the expense of others, but *relationality*: "the wellspring of the felt obligation to take others into account as persons in one's actions." Confucius proclaimed this dictum even before Christ: "Do not impose on others what you yourself do not desire." In that light, good religion always has the right and obligation to confront bad morality. My walk and my talk are driven by the conviction that all children of this global village are my brothers and sisters, and those relationships are meant to be governed by love. Does the crux of the matter lie in what I know, or in the way I walk? Can someone walk in truth on a different path? Is *every* way that leads to truth and life the way of Jesus? That's the way I lean.

> Jesus, keep my heart true. I have not found contentment. I hope that I am now leaning towards that point in my relationship with God where I will find greater peace – a peace that does not let the tendencies of religious separatism trump relationship; a peace tendered by love, but not lost to unfettered relativism. Amen.

The Waiting Is Killing Me

Thus says the Lord: Maintain justice, and do what is right, for soon my salvation will come, and my deliverance be revealed. Isaiah 56:1

They, like me, were growing weary of waiting. They, like me, were waiting for trust to be restored, so they could believe again in someone who deserved their absolute allegiance. Did they, like me, fight dragons of doubt? Was their dragon winning? Perhaps they were losing hope and had shifted into a "maintenance mode" of seeking justice and doing right – not because they still clung to the strong conviction that an ultimate divine consummation was immanent, but simply because they had determined to do what was right. They had followed that right path for so long while wrapped in the blanket of hope, that when the comforter's warmth no longer sheltered their cold shoulders, they nevertheless continued to live as they had done for years. The channels of righteousness had been cut so deep into their communal psyche that the waters of right living just followed the paths of least resistance.

Isaiah offered the hope of deliverance from his people's captivity: a direct divine intervention that would save the people and return them to their Promised Land. All I really want to know and believe, moment by moment, is that God is and that God is relevant. While waiting, I maintain. I know no other way to live. I weary of doing right, but wrong would be the death of me.

> *There are those times, O God, when I come dangerously close to a depth of doubting in which I want to throw up my hands and say, "the hell with clinging to the right." For heaven's sake don't let me die. Amen.*

Postscript

Formative Guilt

Could it be that some of my doubts about God's love are grounded in the angst of non-acceptance during my early and formative years, more than in purely theological misgivings? Do I experience false guilt and feelings of personal inadequacy as a result of how I perceived my parents' expectations – and the heavenly Father's? Are there some childish, core beliefs about self, God, and others that I need to put away through a process of spiritual maturation?

The other day my brother Dave and I got together for our annual "how is it with your soul" pow-wow. He is three years my elder. We reminisced about our childhood conceptions of God. In contrast to the foreboding cloud of eternal doom that hovered over me, Dave always felt love, acceptance, and forgiveness from God. While I often felt my latest slip-up held me dangling over hell's flames, Dave lived in a wonderland of heavenly favor. What accounts for such radically different perceptions?

Dave was born to be a blessing. As he grew "in wisdom and stature," Mom and Dad many times retold the story that would prove to be the formative epic of his life. When he was three years old he suffered a life-threatening disease that typically led either to death or severe brain damage. Our parents and their friends in faith lifted him up before the Almighty. They prayed that if God should graciously spare him, it not be in some vegetative state, but in healthy body and sound mind, fit to fulfill some profound service for God. If he lived, he would be destined for greatness. Well, Dave's life was spared. God loved him and would lead him. He would be sent. My brother swam in this sea of grace, and he knew it. Doubt found no room in this warm manger. Dave had always been the star of our family.

I came along a few years later, the last of seven; not unwanted, but surely unpredicted. Other than their shared desire for godliness, my parents' relationship was faltering. Mom was drowning in the overwhelming responsibilities of family and church, the pain of her broken dream of being a lifetime missionary, and rejection from a husband who pastored with compassion but did not control his sexual passions. Despite his guilt and desire to be holy (as he later confessed to me), Dad could compartmentalize and carry on, seemingly above the fray. I often felt emotional warmth with Mom, but Dad felt distant and disconnected. Mom leaned into a martyr complex, convinced that her trials were tests from God as a means to create a more devoted saint. She prayed constantly, but at times her life was a laborious sigh that fell over the family. I could never fix it. It always found me wonting.

How did they get beyond the pain? They worked harder and sacrificed more. Paradoxically, even as they praised the grace of God, they sought to prove they were worthy of it. They helped many others, but they could not save themselves. My mission was to obey dad and make mom happy. I don't think I did very well with either of those directives. One of mom's common expressions was, "What are people going to think," if we weren't good enough, if we didn't sacrifice more than enough, or if we enjoyed life's good things too much? Even if one of us deserved praise, Dad in particular would not celebrate it. Praise ignited *pride*, which could induce the anger of a jealous God. Believe me, I knew too well how it went down for little boys who did not obey (read: honor and make happy) their parents, and thus fell out of God's grace. For me, it was inadequacy, shame, and guilt. So, in contrast to my brother, there was no warm bosom of God cradling me. I was like the sinner of Johnathan Edwards' famed sermon: hanging by a thread over hell fire. Oh, I was a good kid. But never did I feel affirmed or accepted. I was exhausted and frightened, and just kept smiling because that's what Christians do.

Dad's impassioned desire to be holy was driven by temptation. And more than any of the siblings, I felt the impact of his lapses. This made my task of mothering Mom all the more difficult. During my formative years, Dad was also deeply invested in the "what would people think" mode. He did not express it as frequently as Mom did, speaking, as he usually did, softly; but he carried a big stick. On numerous occasions I took the brunt of his concealed anger, because I behaved in ways that did not reflect proper consideration of what people would think. Sometimes the spankings were due to my conduct at church. Being the pastor, Dad felt strongly that his children should exemplify the best behavior. I was spanked for not sitting properly, for running outside the church building, and for kicking a Sunday School buddy under the table – a false accusation. Why did Dad believe that boy rather than me? Such punishments proclaimed that God was more about guilt than grace.

I did not experience Dad as a loving father. This makes perfect sense in light of the fact that I was enmeshed with my mother during the very years Dad was distancing himself from her. To leave the one was to leave the other. I felt abandoned by one, imprisoned by the other, and left with the legacy to love a God who claimed that I was "guilty as charged." Three strikes and you're out.

Brother Dave's stardom was warranted: he found success in every aspect of his life. That wasn't my story. One time, Dad was frustrated because I could not grasp an Algebra assignment.

"You are never going to be anything, are you!"

These words fell just once, but they fell like Thor's hammer. A high school friend once referred to me as the black sheep of the Leaman family. Did God give a damn about black sheep? If Dave was a rock, standing confident and firm, I was a wind-blown leaf. Even now, our spiritual journeys reflect the contrast.

To Be Saved or Salvaged?

For the grace of God has appeared, bringing salvation to all, training us to renounce impiety and worldly passions, and in the present age to live lives that are self-controlled, upright, and godly, while we wait for the blessed hope and the manifestation of the glory of our great God and Saviour, Jesus Christ. Titus 2:11-13

Neo, in Brian McClaren's *A New Kind of Christian*, encourages Dan, his disillusioned pastor friend, to "play with Scripture." I was taken aback when I read that. How can you possibly play with the words that seal your fate? Well, I'm feeling a little freer these days, so I would like to replace the word salvation with some derivation of *salvaging*. The local junk yard is that place where one gleans whatever wreckage is worth salvaging. What was lost in the rubbish is found and fashioned for renovation. But parts of me remain so rusted by corroding elements of sin that I cannot salvage them for service to God. I am both humbled and frightened.

I am not interested in merely being saved from something – I want to be salvaged for something. Yet any effort on my part to scour the rust will leave spots untouched. Worse, some of that decay actually looks like life to me. I am standing on quicksand that seems to throb with life between my toes, its gritty movement shocking every nerve to life, even as it slowly envelops me in death.

Neither God, nor prayer, nor self-effort can salvage me. Prayer may mitigate guilt, but ultimately it will become a façade for insincerity. But will I die for the sake of what I think I deserve? Certainly not by my will. By my will, I cannot die for any reason – even in order to be raised to new life. Salvation rests with the grace of God; my *salvaging* upon the one who will hold me accountable, to whom my heart is knit. If I am to be salvaged, I must take seriously James 5:16: "Share one another's burdens, so that you might be healed." Sometimes, the blessed hope can be so practical that it hurts.

> *My capacity to forget and forego wisdom frightens me, O God. My own darkness is more daunting than reason permitted. Sin stands at the door and I do not have within me the fortitude to take flight from its allure. Thank you for that brother in Christ who holds me accountable and strengthens my weakened knees. Amen.*

Postscript
Life Would Die on Her Lips

She has been a periodic topic of discussion with my mentor. From the moment we met, I have had to fight a strong, visceral desire to draw her close. Once, I asked a friend to call me in the middle of a professional conference with this woman, just to check my thoughts – temptation is diminished with accountability. But fantasy's fire is not easily extinguished. Today, I still want to kiss her. It is as though her kiss could succor all life's anxiety, affirm my masculinity, and quell the anxieties of growing old. It is not difficult to convince myself that a rendezvous with her would be a well-deserved reward for one who has made a vocation of righteous living.

Years ago I read a novel by Father Capon entitled *Between Noon and Three*. The crux of the book is the question of whether or not the reader would have an ongoing noon-to-three romantic affair if he knew without a doubt that no one would ever find out, and that there would be no negative ramifications for his marriage. I have rehearsed that script, and confess the lure of that caprice. It is disconcerting to acknowledge that, given the right signals and opportunity, the fear of getting caught rather than faithfulness to wife and family would be what holds me back. Fortunately, an additional safety net is that a life of integrity precedes the moment of temptation. Violating that life-witness would lessen my standing even with this woman. Ah, but perhaps she inwardly wants to take a good man down. Perhaps she longs to tear the veil of trust that thinly separates genuine appreciation from raw passion? Love runs deep in my marriage, but temptation does not seem to be conditioned by anything other than the allure of the moment. It is in the milliseconds of each moment that I must remind myself whose I am, and what I am about. My life would die on her lips.

What Do I Lack?

Written on Valentine's Day 2011

The young man said to him, "I have kept all these; what do I still lack?" Jesus said to him, "If you wish to be perfect, go, sell your possessions, and give the money to the poor, and you will have treasure in heaven; then come, follow me."
Matthew 19:20-21

Sometimes the words of that young man fall from these aging lips as well: "What do I still lack? I mean, really, Jesus, after all I have given up for God, what else must I do?"

Regardless of what God gets, The Holy always hollers for more. It takes a helluvah lot of giving for heaven to grant a, "Well, done thy good and faithful servant!" I usually end-up apologizing for the insensitive nature of my gift-giving: "Oh, I'm sorry – I thought you said you preferred white chocolate because it's better for you." "God, I apologize, I thought about this a lot, but how could I know that you wanted the candy heart with 'forever yours' instead of 'be mine?'" "Oh, my bad. Should have known you feel more precious when the envelope is sealed with a bunch of XXXOOOs on the back instead of 'to my sweets' on the front." All the "I'll be sure to get it right, next times" are inevitably the wrong words to say. Didn't I ever read God's Word? I should have known!

There is never any place for the swagger of self-accomplishment most atonement theologies that portray God as an angry and jealous parent. To stand in front of him is to be reminded of John Calvin's assessment of the human being as a "five-foot worm." (People were a bit shorter in those days, which was a lucky thing for them: the length of their sin-filled slime was five inches less than my own offensiveness to the Creator.) Fortunately for me, Calvin doesn't have the final word, Jesus does. To stand face-to-face with Jesus is to hear, "Come unto me all who labor and are heavy-burdened. I will give you rest. My yoke is easy; my burden is light" (Matthew 11:29). These aging lips do not ask the young man's question with the intensity or frequency of years past. I am able to simply *be*. And in Jesus, I can be loved. Life has lightened-up a bit.

> *Dear Jesus, continue to loosen the tethers of a guilt-laden life, so that I might grow in grace. Amen.*

What Is Your Life?

Indeed we call blessed those who showed endurance. You have heard of the endurance of Job, and you have seen the purpose of the Lord, how the Lord is compassionate and merciful. James 5:11

"What is your life? You are a mist that appears for a little while and then vanishes" (James 4:15). James puts life in perspective. Live like death is just around the corner. Be sure you do not waste your time majoring in the minors, for in doing so ongoing anxiety will be your lot. Ultimately, the peace you hope to keep in your bottle of time will evade you, both now and when you journey to the other side. It is evident in chapters four and five that James believes his days are the last days, and that Jesus will soon come again. James warns the rich that they are betting on a losing lifestyle. You may have mined the world's riches, and set security systems in your mansions to guard it, but "misery is coming to you." God hears the voice of the oppressed.

In the meantime, James challenges poor and oppressed believers to wait patiently and resist the grumbling that often accompanies the disenchantment of hopes deferred. He assures them that "the Lord is near," so they should exemplify the patience of Job. As a matter of fact, they'd better watch out . . . "the judge is standing at the door." There should be no crying, doubting, or pouting coming from their corner of the ring. For even if they catch the brunt end of a knock-out punch, the next moment of consciousness will find them shouting with the saints in glory. Ultimately, they will see that the Lord is "full of compassion and mercy." He encourages them to persevere. Legend has it that James was a shining exemplar of persevering faith: he was flayed like a fish.

Sometimes I cry with the Psalmist, "how long, O Lord, how long?" Sadly, it has been so long that I no longer hold a deep conviction that a second coming will happen. My pouting is turning to doubting, and doubting to disbelief. It must have been much easier to live under the expectation of the Almighty's imminent climactic invasion within in the short span from Jesus' walk on earth to the writings of James. Even the Apostle Paul had to find a fitting rationale for the delay of the second coming, in order to cover the sense of immediacy he earlier expressed in his letter to the Thessalonians.

And here we are some 2,000 years later, clinging to a hope molded by the expectations of the early church. Yes, with James I can say "the Lord is near," because the Spirit of God is ever-present in every situation; so, in a sense, God comes again and again and again. That's the meaning I give the liturgy in I celebrate the Lord's Supper: *Christ has died; Christ is risen; Christ will come again.* Yet I know that interpretation falls far short of the strong conviction a believer "should" maintain. I do believe that my life is mist, and I do believe that the Lord is in the midst, and I do believe that God and goodness ultimately win the day: but does that happen as a kind of invasion on a day of redemption when Jesus returns, or as a process of ongoing creative development? I long for the former because it galvanizes hope, and puts redemption completely in the hands of the Deity who created the game and shuffles the deck – not the players who can only follow the rules.

Yet, there are so many more billions suffering today on a daily basis than when this seed of hope was planted! How can a compassionate deity, who knows that humanity cannot redeem itself, continue to shuffle that deck while the world cries out with suffering – which is no game? That question is the seed for my doubt.

How long, O Lord? Amen.

Who Is the Judge?

You shall not pervert the justice due to your poor in their lawsuits. Keep far from a false charge, and do not kill the innocent or those in the right, for I will not acquit the guilty.
Exodus 23:6-7

Who has the final verdict? One of the characters in *The Brothers Karamazov* states: "If God does not exist, then everything is permitted." Yet this text tells us that there is an ultimate authority who establishes the measure of justice. Ultimately, that measure is love. If love can be defined as thoughts and actions that seek the welfare of the other, then to love the other is to love God, and to love myself. Both Islam and Judaism hold to the dictum that to kill one is to kill all. To harm one, is to harm all – including myself.

Will God someday litigate every action? If those who have wronged others are not punished in their own lifetimes, will God get them in the end? Is God, as atheist Richard Dawkins rightfully mocks, like a huge computer, simultaneously surveying the minds and movement of six billion people, while marking a ledger for future courtroom hearings? Or is the judgment of God mediated through some karmic "you reap what you sow" consequences in our lives here and now? Or could it be that, as Rob Bell suggests in his book *Love Wins*, God will ultimately acquit the guilty, and allow Jesus' proclamation of forgiveness on the cross be the final word for every person?

Jesus, amidst so many questions, my prayer is that the answers be wrapped in love. Amen.

Why Worry? A Twinkle of Eternity

Do not worry about anything, but in everything by prayer and supplication with thanksgiving let your requests be made known to God. And the peace of God, which surpasses all understanding, will guard your hearts and your minds in Christ Jesus. Philippians 4:6-7

I memorized this verse years ago, and it has planted many seeds of peace in the face of panic. Despite doubts I am drawn to solace. Somehow this passage speaks to the kind of freedom I experience when I think, "it ain't all up to me." Some time ago in a discussion about prayer with one of my sons, I affirmed Buddhist meditation. My son noted that while meditation brings one into deeper connectedness with all of life, he still finds greater peace in believing that there really is a God beyond the sum of human community. I agree. While Buddhism has broadened my capacity to stay in the moment, because each moment is the only one we can immediately do anything about, I remain bound by my longing to belong to someone greater than myself.

A sanctuary of Tiffany stained glass, splaying light into rays of color; a tree-studded canopy sheltering a lone, tiny bird that sings beside a trickling stream: images of quiet that come to me from that place where heart and mind are quickened to hear the voice that beckons from beyond. To pause in this place, to attune to that voice, is to recall the answered prayers, the gifts received, and the peace that passes understanding. At a depth so much deeper than this solitary soul can traverse alone, and all things do pass, yet all is well. The following poem is a response to the walk in the woods, the singing bird, the trickling stream, and the celebration of the eternal in which we participate every day.

A Twinkle of Eternity

I didn't walk far, but it sure was long
I didn't know a note, but I still sang the song
I didn't catch that star, I just danced amidst the skies
And in sweet time eternity
Became the twinkle in my eyes.

Dear Jesus, I am filled with presence. Stay my mind and my heart upon you. In you I find my peace. Amen.

Wisdom in Foolishness

Give instruction to the wise, and they will become wiser still; teach the righteous and they will gain in learning. The fear of the Lord is the beginning of wisdom, and the knowledge of the Holy One is insight. Proverbs 9:9-10

If one wishes to be nobody's fool, it is wise to seek God's face. But know: this is an ongoing journey. It holds the prospect even for the wise of becoming "wiser still." In the joyful adventure of knowing God, our hearts and minds are transformed, and fulfillment grows as we learn the wisdom of resisting the temptation to "major in the minors." Our society values material gain over relational wholeness with others and God, and the pursuit of wisdom appears foolish. But I cannot make this observation from a place of uppity self-righteousness. I make it, rather, with chagrin at the wide chasm that separates this biblical wisdom from our contemporary reality. Nearly every day I am reminded of this gulf.

O God of Wisdom, foolishly stand by my side when I would conform to the ways of the world around me rather than be transformed by the renewing winds of your Spirit. Make such light of my weakness that, despite any present denial on my part, you know my only hope is in you. Then my fear of you will not be a quaking in your presence, but a heart-warming awe. Amen.

Women and Men of God

Remember your leaders, those who spoke the word of God to you; consider the outcome of their way of life, and imitate their faith. Hebrews 13:7

Men and women of God were: those who valued virtue over personal gain; those who ventured higher, deeper, and broader than the borders of ego-centered existence; those who knew you didn't have to like someone, but you had to love him; those whose vengeance was tempered by forgiveness; those who could seek justice and liberty for the oppressed as well as the oppressor; those who could hold tightly, yet let go freely; those who lived their passions compassionately; those who risked without thought of reward; those who were still long enough to quiet raging storms, and stayed long enough to nurture intimacy; those of gentle spirit who with soft voice spoke strong words; those who knew that the pointed finger is a projection of the pointer; those who were as strong as the oak yet flexible as the palm tree; those who could see both the prodigal and the brother in themselves; those who did not give what was deserved but what was needed; those who died many times to live again. Their way of life was the way of the eternal. Their lives spoke the word of God. Imitate their faith. There is no better way to live.

> *God, I pray that I might live like that woman; that man. Amen.*

Epilogue: July 13, 2017

"Mr. Leaman, you have to breathe. Take a deep long breath, Melvin." The monitor that measured my post-op breathing beeped for the umpteenth time. Once again, nurse Mar called out the reminder. I shared with her that I was really feeling quite content, and that my light breathing was merely a mark of inner meditation.

"I wondered. I saw that book you put into your bag of belongings when you came in this morning. It was something about Mother Teresa." Little did I know that the ensuing dialogue about Mother Teresa with a nurse embarking upon a new Christian pilgrimage, would be a transformative moment for me. "You know, I was raised Buddhist, but just five years ago I became a Christian. I still have so many questions."

"Questions," I said, "is what Mother Teresa's book, and much of my adult life, is all about." I explained that the book in my bag was comprised of the late Saint of Calcutta's private writings. On numerous occasions Mother Teresa had told her spiritual directors to destroy them, but in their wisdom they published them posthumously, under the title of *Mother Teresa: Come Be My Light*. I was reading them for the first time. They were about her darkness, her doubts, and the distance she felt from God even while living every moment for God.

> "The place of God in my soul is blank. There is no God in me. Heaven – souls – why these are just words that mean nothing to me" (p.210)

> "In my soul I feel just that terrible pain of loss – of God not wanting me – of God not being God – of God not really existing (Jesus please forgive my blasphemies) – I am afraid

to write all those terrible things that pass in my soul – I do not pray any longer" (p.193).

I have long felt drawn by the Buddhist perspective, and was intrigued by Mar, this post-Buddhist nurse. What gave her the courage to step beyond family beliefs and legacies and fall into the arms of God? Was it a defining moment, a particular verse, or a friend?

"Oh," she said, "it was the creation story. Buddhism doesn't have a creation story." Well, that much I knew, but what was it about the biblical creation account that caught her?

"Love," she said. "That story tells me I am loved, I belong, I have a creator who cares, and I have purpose." And so it was that as she told her story, the simplicity of love, the necessity of belonging, the integrity of a transforming call to relationship brought us both to tears.

I told her about this book – the one you are now about to close - how I, like Mother Teresa, "struggled with a fear of deceiving others," how I am still far too shallow to know either the depths of love or the "dark nights of the soul" that Mother Teresa experienced. Yet, in faith Mother determined that despite all her questions, her ultimate desire was to quench the "thirst of Jesus – not for water, but for love, for sacrifice."

Mar wants to read my reflections on faith and doubt. But I doubt she realizes the breadth of "faith for faith" (Romans 1:17) she is stirring in me. She has given me this Epilogue.

Let me die with questions; let me live in love.
Mr. Leaman, "Take a long, deep breath."
Amen . . .

Made in the USA
Middletown, DE
09 March 2019